Mapping the Private Geography

Mapping the Private Geography

Autobiography, Identity, and America

GERRI REAVES

McFarland & Company, Inc., Publishers
Jefferson, North Carolina, and London

Acknowledgments: I am grateful to the following expert readers, critics, and editors for their valuable support during my writing process, which began with my graduate work at the University of Miami: Shari Benstock, James Brock, Tassie Gwilliam, Lindsey Tucker, Peter Bellis, Suzanne Ferriss, and Barbara Woshinsky. I would also like to recognize the National Endowment for the Humanities for a fellowship to attend the 1994 Summer Seminar for College Teachers, directed by James Olney and convened at Louisiana State University. During my years at West Virginia Wesleyan College, I relied on the collegial support of Cathy Parker, Janne Abrero, and Sue Roth, all of the Annie M. Pfeiffer Library. My thanks go to them, and to the college for a 1996 Faculty Innovation Grant. And, my sincerest gratitude to Lina and Ursula.

Library of Congress Cataloguing-in-Publication Data

Reaves, Gerri, 1951–
    Mapping the private geography : autobiography, identity, and America / Gerri Reaves.
      p. cm.
    Includes bibliographical references and index.
    ISBN 0-7864-0877-4 (softcover : 60# alkaline paper) ∞
    1. American prose literature — 20th century — History and criticism.   2. Authors, American — Biography — History and criticism.   3. National characteristics, American, in literature. 4. Identity in literature.   5. Stein, Gertrude, 1874–1946. 6. Hellman, Lillian, 1906–   7. Shepard, Sam, 1943– 8. Didion, Joan.   9. Autobiography.   I. Title.
    PS366.A88 R4   2001
    818'.50809 — dc21
    [B]   00-49013

British Library cataloguing data are available

Cover image ©2000 Artville

Manufactured in the United States of America

McFarland & Company, Inc., Publishers
  Box 611, Jefferson, North Carolina 28640
  www.mcfarlandpub.com

Contents

List of Abbreviations

I have adopted the following abbreviations for works cited in the text. Complete publication information for the editions cited appears in Works Cited and Consulted.

Joan Didion

AH	*After Henry*
BCP	*A Book of Common Prayer*
Play	*Play It As It Lays*
STB	*Slouching Toward Bethlehem*
WA	*The White Album*

Gertrude Stein

ABT	*The Autobiography of Alice B. Toklas*
EA	*Everybody's Autobiography*
HWW	*How Writing Is Written*
PF	*Paris France*
TI	"A Transatlantic Inter-view — 1946"
WIHS	*Wars I Have Seen*

Lillian Hellman

M	*Maybe*
P	*Pentimento* (in *Three*)
ST	*Scoundrel Time* (in *Three*)
UW	*An Unfinished Woman* (in *Three*)

Sam Shepard

FFL	*Fool for Love*
MC	*Motel Chronicles*
RTL	*Rolling Thunder Logbook*

American Identity: The Personal Is the Geographical

> Gatsby believed in the green light, the orgiastic future
> that year by year recedes before us. It eluded us then, but
> that's no matter — tomorrow we will run faster, stretch out
> our arms farther.... And one fine morning —
> So we beat on, boats against the current, borne back
> ceaselessly into the past.
> — *The Great Gatsby*

Although these lines close an F. Scott Fitzgerald novel, they encapsulate a host of autobiographical metaphors that hinge on geography and mapping as paradigms for self-representation. The metaphors reinforce traditional conceptions of autobiographical texts *and* point out the undoing of those conceptions, an undoing well documented in the last three decades of autobiography studies. A person's life is a line transversing and marking a landscape; life is a sea in which humans are cast adrift; life is a journey with a discernible beginning, middle stages, and a conclusive end; the self is separate from the context of the life — that sea — in which the self is immersed; and life is a current moving toward a logical end. However, the description of Gatsby is also a paradigm for the circularity of memory and the impossibility of mapping; we are "borne back ceaselessly," but can never retrieve what is lost. Despite our intentions to adhere to the current of life, we find ourselves aswirl in that circularity of memory; the order that traditional autobiography imposes on a life has vanished, replaced by a self that exists only textually, and by the confirmation that the genre, too, is as elusive as Gatsby's "orgiastic future." The inevitable undoing of autobiography lies in its own accomplishment.

The three twentieth-century American autobiographies that are the focus of this book reside on the shifting boundary between individual and collective American identity: Gertrude Stein's *Everybody's Autobiography* (1937), Lillian Hellman's *Scoundrel Time* (1976), and Sam Shepard's *Motel Chronicles* (1982). In the following chapters, I trace three fluctuating, indeterminate, and intertwining components of each text: genre, identity, and place, in this case America. I argue that Stein, Hellman, and Shepard reinvent autobiography, the self, and America in texts that can be defined loosely as travel literature, history, and fragmentary reflections, respectively. These highly idiosyncratic texts exemplify the expansion of autobiography to the degree that it no longer exists as a discrete, stable genre. They also exemplify how autobiographers who adopt a geographical paradigm for the self can simultaneously balance individual identity and agency with often invasive and threatening collective ones. These autobiographical texts reiterate the much-discussed, problematic status of the terms *autobiography* and *self*, and demonstrate the need to add *place* as a third term to the list.

My primary interest is to explore the private geography that constitutes America for Stein, Hellman, and Shepard, and, by extension, to identify elements that have characterized much of American autobiography. I concentrate on the strategies by which these writers invent the self as they rework their familial, cultural, and national engenderings and reconceive America and their Americanism by mapping a private geography — a psychological map, a myth, an ideology, or a fiction. The practice of self-representation requires one to define the emotional, cultural, and psychic landscape in which one conceives that self to exist. In their autobiographical acts, Stein, Hellman, and Shepard reject many of the standard organizing concepts or psychological contexts of autobiography; instead, familial relations and genealogy, history, and common culture often become threats rather than comforts and sources of stability. Thus, they revise the teleology that comprises the given context of identity formation.

Whether an author views America as an ideology, a set of cultural codes, a geographical place, a metaphorical space, a myth, a fiction, or even a state of mind, that vision defines the sense of self and structures an autobiographical discourse. This study, therefore, demands investigation into the questions I introduce in Chapter One: (1) Why do we conceive of selfhood in geographical terms? and (2) What is the significance of the pervasive spatial and geographical metaphors used in autobiographical writings and in the criticism and theory of autobiography as well? What is the significance of the coalescence of physical and metaphorical space? Which alternative paradigms for self-definition emerge when we cease to view the American autobiographical act as something contained, accomplished, and complete?

America as myth or idea supersedes its identity as a geographical reality, whether envisioned as a desert paradise, a purifying wilderness, a theocratic garden of God, or the redemptive West.[1] Leonard Lutwack points out that from the beginning of the European settlement of America, the "ideal was more important than the actual place in which it was to be realized" (143). On the one hand, Stein and Hellman participate in the tradition Sacvan Bercovitch labels "auto-American-biography: the celebration of the representative self as America, and of the American self as the embodiment of a prophetic universal design" (*Puritan* 136). Their prophetic works envision an ideal nation and continue the tradition of "vicarious national autobiography" that originated with Whitman's *Leaves of Grass* (Sayre 252).[2] On the other hand, they demonstrate William Boelhower's theory that American identity, like America itself, is an abstract idea (75). Having lost our sense of place, we have become a "nation of strangers" (Turri qtd. in Boelhower 75). America is on the road and the road is a "non-place" where, increasingly, the geographical translates into the abstract (74). Even Jean Baudrillard, from his fascinated, non–American point of view, describes America as "a hyperreality"; "America is neither dream nor reality" (28). Like Stein, who generalizes about American character based on her observations regarding road signs and architecture (e.g., windows and fences), he extrapolates universal truths from the particulars of popular culture: "information concerning the whole is contained in each of its elements" (29). For Stein, Hellman, and Shepard, America constitutes the internalized, cultural geography where identity and place meet, the abstract territory where American autobiographical identity originates.

Chapter One of this study examines the repercussions in autobiography studies of what Sidonie Smith calls the end of metaphysical selfhood. This questioning of traditional assumptions about the unitary self of traditional autobiography frames my overview of the crisis in autobiography studies, which focuses on authority, truth, and the stability and coherence of the subject/author. Drawing on current theory of identity politics, this study investigates *place* in autobiography theory, as one of the crucial terms, along with *self* and *text*.

Chapters Two, Three, and Four focus on Stein, Hellman, and Shepard, respectively. Each chapter formulates a fundamental question arising from the nexus of autobiography-selfhood-place and highlights a major issue in autobiography studies. And in highlighting these controversial points in autobiography studies, each text challenges us to consider the role of place in autobiographical writings, to see it as the third axis around which autobiography turns.

Chapter Two addresses Stein's return to the question Who confers identity? as she views the landscape of anxiety that America represents for her. It is simultaneously a mirror confirming her genius and Americanism and a reminder of frightening insecurities and gaps in her memory and identity. Her perpetual worry over whether she is the "I" known by her little dog or the "I" she subjectively experienced symbolizes her struggle to reconcile two differing and inescapable definitions of her self.

Chapter Two also considers Stein's statement "Anything is an autobiography" (*EA* 5), which foreshadows the definitional dilemmas that would face autobiography studies in the coming decades. As she chronicles her 1934-1935 American tour, her only return to her native country between her expatriation in 1904 and her death in 1946, she redefines the genre to reflect her view that time, memory, and public recognition interfere with the creative process and the attainment of genius. In trying to escape retrospective narrative and identity, the expressions of time and self in traditional autobiography, she articulates her own philosophical premises of time and self: her "continuous present" merges the acts of composition and reading, and "entity" signifies the self that transcends the limitations of ordinary time and lives in the moment of writing.

Stein envisions herself as the personification of Americanism, writing "I am clear I am a good American" (*EA* 301). She is the generic "everybody" of the title *and* the unique individual who writes the text. *Everybody's Autobiography* is a catalogue of comments on American streets, houses, art, food, books, everyday habits, windows, road signs, and so on. Her adamant and unconventional definitions of her own Americanism and America conflate: America's physical, psychological, and political traits describe herself. She works backwards genealogically, reinterpreting her past experiences and inventing a teleology to explain and justify herself as a self-created literary genius, exile, and public phenomenon of the modernist age.

Everybody's Autobiography does end with an ostensible reconciliation of the private and public selves, entity and identity. Stein the celebrity at last seems at home with the unsettling and threatening aspects of celebrity status. But does Stein genuinely intend to reconcile the self she re-encounters on the American landscape with the self she has created in exile? Is the book's close a "desperate shoring-up of the reflected image against disintegration and division" (Benstock, "Authorizing" 15) she perceives in the mirror that is her American landscape of anxiety? Or is the reconciliation announced on the final page of her text just another brilliant and surprising Steinian move, a parody of the self-knowledge and closure found in traditional autobiography? She writes, "Perhaps I am not I, even if my little dog knows me but anyway I like what I have and now it is today" (EA 318).

Chapter Three explores Hellman's implicit question, Who owns memory?, the motivation behind her insistence on rewriting American history. The power of Hellman's text hinges on her dramatic insistence that the authority of her personal memory — what I call the ownership of memory — takes precedence over and unquestionably exceeds in authority the historical, collective memory of her critics and peers.[3]

Hellman, rather than duplicating Stein's overt challenge to the genre, masquerades Scoundrel Time as a traditional memoir. It covertly exploits genre expectations, however, and expertly uses italicized subtexts to elevate subjective experience to the status of objective history. Hellman's "memoir" — a word she chooses by default to describe her autobiographical projects — appears, superficially, to be a conventional historical memoir. However, she takes full advantage of the analogy between history and autobiography, between historical and personal narratives, to accomplish personal ends in a public and politically charged fashion.

Hellman appoints herself America's official rememberer and private historian, public and political roles Stein categorically rejects, to assure that America's tendency to forget will not doom it once again to the disgrace signified by the House Un-American Activities Committee (HUAC) and Watergate. Hellman refuses to surrender control over the construct of the author and deals with the burden of the past and memory by designing her text so that she never relinquishes control of it; she adds overlays and italicized commentary in 1979 to Three (An Unfinished Woman [1969] and Pentimento [1973] included as well). The additions, or subtexts,[4] of her palimpsest subvert a definitive interpretation of her ethics or role in the McCarthy hearings. But they give her the powerful option to revise personal and political opinions and to reinterject herself into the ongoing controversy about her memoirs. In these subtexts, she remains a presence to be reckoned with as she maintains a commentator's — not only an autobiographer's — role in her own text.

Scoundrel Time demonstrates in the extreme the political possibilities of an autobiographical text as a space of "rupture and resistance" (S. Smith, "Self" 17). Like Stein's *Everybody's Autobiography*, *Scoundrel Time* effectively privileges personal motives and subjective memory over genre authority and public expectations. Hellman endows an omnipotent, unquestioned authority to both the memoirist and her subjective truth.[5] While Stein's signature becomes synonymous with literary genius, Hellman's represents American heroism.

Chapter Four analyzes Shepard's apparent sidestepping of the issue of genre altogether in *Motel Chronicles*, a move that contrasts provocatively with Hellman's appropriation of an absolutist, ultra-confident authority. Shepard explores the question What are the possibilities of identity? as he disperses and diminishes rather than extends his authorial role. He effaces his public image by exploring a vulnerable plural identity, what he calls a "galaxy" of selves. His evasive authorship produces a fractured, fragmented text that avoids what is traditionally a desirable goal of autobiography: historicizing a coherent, unified self. Like Stein, he displays "an unfixed repertoire of many subject positions" (Paul Smith 107), registering the discrepancy between the false unity of the textual "I" and the subjective experience of the plural self. Shepard offers "a model of nonrepresentative, dispersed, displaced subjectivity" that borrows from his theories on fictional characters in his plays (Brodzki and Schenck 6). In this sense, *Motel Chronicles*'s decentered subject is an example of the feminized subject, lacking the unidirectionality (Jelinek, "Introduction" 17) that certain feminist critics attribute to traditional autobiography and men's lives.[6] Shepard's text resists essentialist readings. But, as a paradoxical examination of selfhood that enacts the deconstruction of the unitary self, *Motel Chronicles* points the direction for a post–World War II genre in rebellion against itself. Shepard suggests that contemporary Americans experience America less as a geographical or political absolute than as a fragmented cultural and ideological context.

The America of Sam Shepard is contradictory. He contemplates the American landscape and its stillness with a nearly religious reverence, but expresses the futility of permanently finding home; this reverence does not resemble the intense connection to the physical landscape that both Stein and Hellman clearly feel. Oddly, Stein the exile remains remarkably attached to her homeland, and Hellman's connection to the idealized landscape of her Hardscrabble Farm in Upstate New York affirms her patriotism, her devotion to an old-fashioned American way of life. But for Shepard, America is a combination of the psychic release found in the myth of the frontier and the West — the freedom of the American male wandering on an endless landscape — and a frustrating maze. *Motel Chronicles* is actually a collection of genres: poems, narratives, fragments, photographs, fiction, autobiography, and biography. It is a casebook of American contemporary culture — from Hollywood movies to the 1960s' counterculture. The text's fragmentation physically mirrors the displacement resulting from pervasive American emotional and cultural disorientation. *Motel Chronicles* textually duplicates that maze: the fragmented text resembles an America defined by the road culture — an endless crisscrossing, a circuitry that ignores boundaries and leads only to itself. The text's narrative direction endlessly folds back on itself, denying the linearity and endless space promised by the myth of the West. *Motel Chronicles* underscores that Shepard's real, twentieth-century America denies him the optimistic vision inherent in the myth of Bercovitch's "redemptive West" (186): an open and promising landscape whose meaning derives from and satisfies human needs. For Shepard, the open space of the American West does not spell freedom and effective agency.

The study concludes by examining the implications of this study for American self-representation in general. Analysis of Joan Didion's America — a "projection on air, a kind of hologram" — reveals hers as the latest and definitive vision for an America that transcends geography. Her America is no longer predicated on stable geographical or cultural terms. Like Stein, Hellman, and Shepard, she maps a new intersection at which genre, self, and place meet: a nexus for the disintegrated genre, the poststructuralist self, and an awareness of the roles geography and mapping play in defining the autobiographical project.

Didion's work, as a culminating example, defines the consequences of dis-placement, of our tenuous hold on the tangibility of American geography. Her look at late twentieth-century America helps us approach the questions that Stein, Hellman, and Shepard foreground: What does it mean to relinquish the ideological certainties so central to Stein's and Hellman's Americas and to embrace the indeterminate and unsettling America of Shepard? In what ways is our sense of self and Americanism shaped when we sit before our computers, crawl into cyberspace, a world in which geographical reality is all but irrelevant? In the early twenty-first century, we confront the erasure of all boundaries that organize, limit, and confine us; "even the boundaries between Space and Outer Space are not binding any more" (Mohanty qtd. in Kirby 187). Will we eventually conceive of life as taking place in "time-space," as Leonard Lutwack phrases it, "and overcome the tyranny of place" (237)? Which of the contradictory definitions of America will triumph? Freedom, or placelessness and the attendant alienation?

CHAPTER ONE

Definitional Dilemmas in Autobiography Studies: Self, Genre, and Place

It is not down in any map; true places never are.
—*Moby Dick*

Autobiographical theory of the last three decades documents the unraveling of traditional assumptions about the textual representation of the self.[1] Leah D. Hewitt concisely defines the generic assumptions about selfhood and language implicitly questioned by Stein, Hellman, and Shepard and many other twentieth-century autobiographers:

> The traditional view of autobiography ... grounds itself in the metaphysics of the conscious, coherent, individual subject. Language in this perspective is a tool to represent faithfully the already extant self and the past life. In the second half of the twentieth century, this conception of autobiography has, of course, radically changed (and was, no doubt, always already being challenged in practice): the "individual's" autonomy, with its concomitant social and linguistic authority, has been seriously eroded. The text now creates the fictions of a "self" rather than the reverse [3].

Poststructuralism has brought with it the end of that fictional self, the end of "metaphysical selfhood" ("Self" 11), as Sidonie Smith terms it. And con-

current with the demise of the post–Englightenment self is the disappearance of that "unitary, irreducible, atomic ... Cartesian self, its vision ...
rational, totalizing, and appropriative ... its movement through time teleological" (S. Smith, "Self" 11). The self is now a subject and is the "site of
dialogue with the world, others, memory, experience, and the unconscious"
("Self" 15). Three-dimensional metaphors for the postmodern, unfettered
subject abound and announce the multiple, often contradictory, nature of
that subject. It is "implicated in sinuous webs of intersubjectivity," a position potentially empowering or "enslaving" ("Self" 15–16).[2] Leigh Gilmore's
terms for the autobiographical subject, "axis of identity, ... the intersection of the universal and the particular," and "network of differences"
(*Autobiographics* 184, 185), reconfigure our conceptions of the unitary "I"
in poststructuralist terms and alert us to what Betty Bergland labels the
"travesty" (162) of the unified, coherent autobiographical subject.

   The texts examined here confront the impossibility of writing autobiography in the traditional sense, with a stable, coherent subject and an
author who is the repository of truth about the subject. For Stein,
Rousseau's "concepts of subject, self, and author as independent sover-
eignties" (Sprinker 326) collapse into a single process and herald the
supremacy of the writing act itself (Sprinker 342). Shepard's *Motel Chronicles*, like *Everybody's Autobiography*, revises Rousseau's holy trinity of
independent subject, self, and author, each able to stand in judgment on
the other in a suspended objectivity. The works of Stein, Hellman, and
Shepard exemplify that reversal in perspective that Paul de Man alludes
to: the "interest of autobiography ... is not that it reveals reliable self-
knowledge ... but that it demonstrates ... the impossibility of closure and
of totalization ... of all textual systems made up of tropological substitu-
tions" (922). This impossibility transforms autobiography; once endowed
with authority through its association with history, it is now just another
text. The genre, along with the autobiographical self, is "threatened with
generic extinction" (S. Smith, "Self" 17). The neologism "life writing,"
which includes not only autobiography but biography, journals, memoirs,
tell-all/exposé autobiographies (termed "hot art" by Ellen Goodman), letters, personal criticism (a blending of academic scholarship and the autobiographical), creative nonfiction, and a host of other genres difficult to
categorize, reflects scholars' need for a more inclusive term to refer to genres that often overlap and defy precise definition.

   What makes the texts of Hellman, Shepard, and especially Stein excellent examples of the *construction* of self is their foregrounding of textual
identity as purely a linguistic effect inevitably at odds with identity as
experienced by the self. Their texts celebrate — indeed, take as subject

matter — the "gaps in the temporal and spatial dimensions" (Benstock, "Authorizing" 19) masked by the seamless effect of traditional autobiography. They bring into relief a central question: Does the self depend upon language for its existence, or does the self exist prior to language?

Theorists and critics have catalogued the problematics of traditional autobiography, calling into question the premise that the self is paradoxically both the origin and the object of the text; that the autobiographical text is an accurate textual mirror; that the self is a unified, stable entity existing through time; and that the author is the sole authority of the text rather than its organizer or fictional construct. Even the reader's right to expect a certain "truth-value," the text's consistency with other evidence (Bruss, "Eye" 299), has been challenged. Hellman's *Scoundrel Time*, for example, demonstrates the confusion that results from the application of the outdated fact-fiction dichotomy, only one dichotomy on which critical approaches to autobiography have depended until recently. Instead, theorists and critics are reaching the consensus that all texts are autobiographical (including literary criticism and scientific writing, for example) and thereby deny the existence of the genre as a discrete category. To redefine autobiography as an expanded genre is not enough; it infiltrates all texts.

Leigh Gilmore bridges poststructuralist and feminist theories when she argues for the term "autobiographics" in her examination of autobiographical writing by women: "It is important to claim autobiography *as a kind of writing and not a genre per se* in order to emphasize further the extent to which women's autobiography invades, permeates, and also is invaded by canonical genres" (*Autobiographics* 41; emphasis added). Labeling autobiography a "discursive hybrid" (17), Gilmore takes a long-overdue theoretical leap by not only announcing the abolishment of autobiography as a discrete genre, but by redefining it as a set of operations that might occur in any text (ix). Rejecting genre definitions derived from Augustine (widely accepted as the origin of autobiography in Western literature), she instead offers a geographical metaphor for the genre, autobiographics, elements which "mark a location in a text where self-invention, self-discovery, and self-representation emerge within the technologies of autobiography — namely, those legalistic, literary, social, and ecclesiastical discourses of truth and identity through which the subject of autobiography is produced" (42). She has in effect answered the clarion call of Domna C. Stanton, E. S. Burt, Paul de Man, and many others, who concur that "the whole project of defining autobiography generically is what needs to be abandoned" (Burt qtd. in Stanton 8). Robert Elbaz suggests defining the genre as "an ideological statement" (9), a subjective statement examining *the possibility* of writing a life rather than the story of a life told by a unified, coherent subject. Traditionally the means for understanding and conveying the meaning of a life, autobiography increasingly functions as the method of that inquiry rather than the answer to it.

Elizabeth Bruss and Shari Benstock point out the usually overlooked ideological and personal investment the reader makes in buttressing and preserving the authority in traditional autobiography. Bruss connects our contemporary condition to the need to keep alive the promise of traditional autobiography: "With so much of life and even identity beyond our personal control, we perhaps cling all the more fiercely to an institution which offers us at least one remaining area of symbolic power over our destiny as individuals" (*Autobiographical* 163-64). Benstock furthers this analysis by specifying exactly who does and does not benefit from the continued denial of poststructuralism's profound impact on autobiography studies and feminist theory. "Those who cling" to the traditional notions of autobiography, she points out, "are those whose assignment under Symbolic law is to *represent* authority, to represent the phallic power that drives inexorably toward unity, identity, sameness" (19). She precisely defines this ideological argument: "And it is not surprising that those who question such authority are those who are expected to submit to it, those who line up on the other side of the sexual divide — that is, women" ("Authorizing" 19-20). If we juxtapose the resistance and anxiety of those who religiously cling to the idea of a discrete, intact genre for ideological certainty against the new possibilities documented in identity politics and embraced by feminist and ethnic studies, we have before us the crisis in autobiography studies.

Reader expectation is at the heart of this late twentieth-century crisis in autobiography studies: the reader's demands are at odds with the nature of the autobiographical text as revealed by poststructuralist and feminist critics. Reading practices are a combination of natural desires for unity and coherence and of learned behaviors inculcated primarily by educational institutions and the marketplace. These desires and learned behaviors dictate the reader's expectations about what an autobiographical text should deliver and how the reader will respond to the text. Autobiography in particular lends itself to such coercive readings. It offers the illusion of ideological certitude, a historical, verifiable narrative that coincides with or reinforces an image of a reality outside the text. The narrative is all the more seductive because it "really happened," the reader believes — how else could it be sold as autobiography? Thus, autobiography, as a subgenre of history, comforts the reader by offering illusory truth, both in terms of objective fact and in the promised profound understanding of a human being's inner life. The reader's usually unacknowledged (even unconscious) demand that the autobiographical text be a mirror of life confirms and bolsters the fiction of a unified, stable identity. This assumed correspondence between the self that writes and the self that is written deceptively equates the *I* of the text with the proper name on the book's title page.

Consequently, the reader's expectations of autobiography are not only greater, but more narrowly defined than those imposed upon other genres, such as novels and films; and the texts of Stein, Hellman, and Shepard highlight the disproportionate, often unconscious expectations of the reader. Behind the expectations lurk the problematic assumptions that autobiography is a sacred, neutral ground, the last bastion of accurate, unbiased narrative. (The fact that autobiography's roots lie in religious confession still shapes the reader's expectations.) Thus, autobiography's apparent historical status leaves it vulnerable to another kind of attack. Readers will tolerate and forgive a degree of inaccuracy or fictionalizing that aesthetically enhances the text, but readers can be very demanding and intolerant when the facts in question conflict or intersect with national, official memories, in other words, history. Is it the reader who insists that the text's historical responsibility is primary? For example, is Hellman obligated to tell the factual truth and nothing but the factual truth about her appearance before the House Un-American Activities Committee? And who decides what qualifies a text for status as validated public memory?

Gilmore's insights into the Anita Hill–Clarence Thomas hearings elucidate this conflict between personal and public truth and questions the authority to define what the going historical truth will be: "[T]he multiple locations of truth within a culture often collide with a single location of the law," she writes, "and it is frequently a hostile place without justice for those whose lives and experiences do not coincide with the preexisting standard for judging truth, eliciting justice, or provoking mercy" (*Autobiographics* 224; footnote). The Hill-Thomas theatre of competing confessions recapitulates in many ways Hellman's experience after the publication of *Scoundrel Time* in 1976: her version of the truth collides with other contradictory and condemnatory versions of her political views and her appearance before HUAC. Her fight for the supremacy of her version of the events epitomizes the tangled mass of truth narratives involved when public and private memories attempt to occupy the same location on the cultural matrix.

Autobiographical studies force questions that extend beyond academic concerns into cultural events, politics, and other arenas. How do we justify attributing great, unquestioned authority to the letters, annotations, and marginalia of canonized authors, when such comments by an unrecognized author would be deemed trivial and lacking in authority? Why the great effort to verify the truth of the former while dismissing the possible importance of the latter? Do we endow the author or the purported truth of the text with the greater authority? Why are some memoirs, such as *Scoundrel Time*, appropriated and virtually rewritten by the public in an outpouring of angry reviews and responses in which the authors attempt to redefine truth in the text, while the authority of less political memoirists goes unquestioned? Is this not an insistence brought by the reader to the text, rather than the text's inherent demand of the reader? And what about texts that claim not to be autobiographical but nevertheless have that status forced upon them by insistent readers with agendas all their own (e.g., D. H. Lawrence's *Sons and Lovers* or James Joyce's *A Portrait of the Artist as a Young Man*)? Or what of the reverse, texts purporting to be autobiographical but condemned as fiction (e.g., Mary McCarthy's *Memoirs of a Catholic Girlhood* or Richard Wright's *Black Boy*), or in the case of Hellman's *Scoundrel Time*, labeled as out and out lies?

Letting go of the myth of the coherent subject endowed with unquestionable authority and of the idea of *genre* allows us to escape the definitional dilemmas, the terminology merry-go-round that diverts our attention from text to taxonomy. Abandoning the thankless and endless jobs of verifying the author's authority and policing the boundaries of autobiography enables us to establish a basis for reading all texts with critical theories that function as reading tools rather than as inflexible containers into which we coercively fit the text and satisfy our need to control it. Abandoning these tasks prevents us from using theory and criticism merely as our own self-confirming mirror.

Place: The Third Term

A better understanding of the roles of spatial metaphors in the autobiographer's sense of self is crucial, given the extent to which *America* and *Americanism* are inevitably bound up with the right to consume space, to move freely, to set and cross boundaries at will, to command and own space — ultimately, to mark space, to inscribe the landscape; the extent to which textual metaphors overlap with geographical ones; and the extent to which the autobiographical act is a seizing of territory, a taking of textual space. What does one's spatial or geographical existence have to do with identity boundaries, difference, identity formation, separation, and anxiety — i.e., with autobiography itself? We must conceive of place in infancy, just as we must differentiate between "I" and "other." The birth of a spatial identity is concurrent with the birth of a psychological identity. We conceive of a psychic geography before we place ourselves spatially and draw boundaries between "I" and "not I." Thus, with the birth of the ego and self, the acquisition of language, and the birth of linear time, comes the birth of spatial identity, one's sense of the self in place.

This study treats place as the unstable, undefinable complement to the post-metaphysical self, for place, like self, resists simple formulation. Thus, this study defines *place* as the tangible or intangible, internal or external context for remembered experience, including fictionalized or distorted memories that have gained the status of fact over time. This definition of place includes states of mind (Shepard's "stillness"); idealized, fictionalized scenes (Hellman's "hours of the deer"); mythic scenarios (Shepard's American West); ideologies (Hellman's traditional American moral code); and ideas (the America Stein envisions while absent from it for 31 years).

There is growing recognition that place or geography is not a neutral, invisible aura of experience which accrues outside the self, unentangled from the ideological and psychological complexities of defining a self in an autobiographical text or from defining one's position in a real world complete with political, economic, and personal consequences. Nor is place or geography a discrete and stable site from which we exert our influence. Instead, one's places (and I emphasize the plural) on the grid — Gilmore's "axis of identity" (184) — are undeniably components of both identity and the autobiographical text.

How unconsciously we slide into geographical and spatial language, whether in critical writing or everyday conversation. Critical jargon is replete with words that imply place and space —*situate, reside, groundwork, territory, demarcate, field, boundary, margin, position*— words that require of the writer and reader not only a sense of agency, but a sense of where that agency emanates from. In other words, we place the self on an ideological grid, or on a political or discursive map, in a process Adrienne Rich might call "the politics of location." All writing, especially autobiography, involves placing the textual *I* in a physical context, whether real or invented.

The intersection of place and identity is the obvious starting point for reconceiving the autobiographical subject. Theorists and critics repeatedly rely on geographical language in writings about the politics of identity, in rethinking subjectivity, and in evaluating the subject's political agency. In their reliance on words such as *site* and *body*, which signify a discrete, contained physical self, they expose the stabilizing urges in criticism itself. This subject, I argue, neither capitulates to the disempowered, fragmented poststructuralist self nor nostalgically re-embraces the fictions of metaphysical selfhood.

At this intersection of place and self, assumptions about roles of place and geography in autobiographical writings are highlighted, thus helping us to avoid duplicating problematic assumptions made about self in discussions of place. Kathleen M. Kirby observes that "more and more, theorists are using the language and experience of space to build their arguments and to construct their political approaches" (173).[3] Countering the more dehumanizing aspects of the poststructuralist subject — its shattered, splintered, dispersed, or disintegrated fate — some critics contend that the plural subject instead "might ... provide a site for cultural critique and social change" (Bergland 162). Sidonie Smith argues, in spatial language, for the political potential in envisioning a post-Enlightenment, pluralistic self: "Through the chafings of our conflictual centerings and marginalities and the interplay of our positionalities and mobilities, spaces of rupture and resistance, of reproduction and representation will emerge in our individual and collective webs" ("Self" 17). Leigh Gilmore, too, labels the site of the (autobiographical) subject as a location for political potential: "Autobiographics, as a description of self-representation, and as a reading practice, is concerned with interruptions and eruptions, with resistance and contradiction as strategies of self-representation" (*Autobiographics* 42). Kirby optimistically and rightly envisions in spatial metaphors the next construct for understanding a self that combines poststructuralist possibilities and the valued individualism of humanism: "Space might form the basis for advancing a responsive and responsible model of the subject, one that abandons neither political realities nor personal histories, nor arrests possibilities for change" (189).[4] Such geographical language betrays tacit acknowledgments that a self must necessarily exist in a context, and most important, that we invent the context as we claim subjectivity.

The post-structuralist view of the self as multiple subjectivities relies, oddly enough, on concepts and language that imply a physical self, on an essentialist notion of self. This subjectivity depends on an essentialist concept of place, too, and co-implicates and conjoins the human being's physical experience of place (from the vantage of one's self as body) and one's experience in a figurative landscape, a cultural context. Diana Fuss clarifies the competing or contradictory definitions of self and subjectivity in identity politics: "[T]he essentialism in 'anti-essentialism' inheres in the notion of place or positionality. What is *essential* to social constructionism is precisely this notion of 'where I stand,' of what has come to be called, appropriately enough, 'subject-positions'" (29). This subject-position strips away the binarism, the mutual exclusivity of self and place, and instead makes them interdependent. Self and location work in tandem.[5]

Sidonie Smith also links the concepts of identity and place, the personal and geographical, by focusing on the body as home: "We may even speculate that subjectivity is the elaborate residue of the border politics of the body since bodies locate us topographically, temporally, sociologically as well as linguistically in a series of transcodings alongs [sic] multiple axes of meaning" ("Identity's" 267). She defines subjectivity as a merging of political, physical, personal, and geographical placements, infinitely variable, unpredictable, and therefore unstable.

Contrast these poststructuralist and feminist reconceptions of place with J. Gerald Kennedy's remarks on the dearth of critical work in literary studies that give place sufficient attention: "[A]lthough numerous critical discussions examine time in autobiography, place remains an apparently incidental issue" (*Imagining* 24).[6] He, like a growing number of critics, recognizes the important work of geographers, most notably Edward Relph, planners, sociologists, and other professionals, and predicts positive repercussions in autobiography studies: "[T]o judge from the appearance of several recent titles, literary critics now seem poised to undertake a concerted inquiry into the poetics of place" (*Imagining* xii).[7] Kennedy emphasizes the near impossibility of imagining autobiography without the physical reality of place as the context for human experience ("Place" 512); he, too, conjoins the abstract politics of identity and the real experience of living in the body in a physical setting.

Kathleen Kirby defines the next theoretical move: She invents a self by merging the poststructuralist self and the essentialist self centered in the body. She thus simultaneously renders unproblematic the stable, contained physical self: "Once we have discarded the Enlightenment individual model of the subject as pure disembodied, evanescent, transcendent 'mind,' it is impossible to imagine the subject except in some yet-to-be-specified relation to real space" (174–75).[8] Critical studies of literature focusing on place or geography usually do one or both of the following: First, they assume place to be a tangible, definable, and stable location, the backdrop or setting for the life recounted. Place viewed in this way is the complement to the stable, unitary metaphysical self. Often, this tangible setting symbolizes a significant time period in the autobiographer's life or serves as the landscape onto which the author projects emotions or attitudes. A particular landscape might represent the unknown and threatening; Southern Louisiana the exotic and sensual; the Old South a lost golden Arcadia; the Wilderness a place of both evil and redemption, or in slave narratives, escape, haven, and a temporary relief from oppression; the mountaintop transcendence. Second, the studies might focus on marginalized authors, ethnic, post-colonial, and African-American writers, particularly women. These studies emphasize the connection between where people are "placed" psychically and politically and where they are placed geographically. Bergland argues that the advantages of studying ethnic autobiographies "to understand the multiplicity of subject-positions that constitute a single agent" is that they "enable us to see the concrete effects of multiple discourses in the culture, and thus permit a better understanding of cultural construction of difference" (157). Scholarship on ethnic autobiography inevitably provokes numerous questions about the interplay of identity and geography, questions that map the directions for autobiography studies.[9] To which landscape and culture does a newly arrived immigrant belong? With which map do we associate a post-colonial writer residing in one country but clearly writing in the tradition of and about the birth country? What makes it possible or desirable for someone to transfer allegiance to a new geographical location, to cultivate a sense of belonging? In essence, what does place have to do with one's sense of self?

America and the Invention of Place

Clearly, in addition to interrogating what Elbaz calls "the ontological status of the self," the autobiographical works of Stein, Hellman, and Shepard also question the ontological status of place, "drawing attention to an ineluctable gap between the locus mapped and studied by the geographer and the individual experience of place" (Kennedy, "Place" 497). Stein defines her somewhat mythical America from a great geographical and emotional distance. Hellman's Hardscrabble Farm in New York embodies an ideal America she sees slipping away in the 1950s because of political and general moral corruption. Shepard's American West is both a landscape central to the myth of the American male and a geography that mirrors the split between the paternal and maternal; it is both the exterior landscape on which his displaced and reclusive father lives and the comforting idealized internal landscape of memory which his mother inhabits. In all three works, America substitutes to some extent for the standard organizing categories of autobiography usually measured in linear time or in the spiritual or intellectual progression of the self (e.g., the human life span, a journey, a conversion narrative). The texts examined here expand the text-self dyad, the focus of autobiography theory, to text-self-place, or autobiography-identity-America.

Stein, Hellman, and Shepard remind us not only of the textual quirkiness of autobiography, but of the quirkiness and deconstructive nature of maps, which are, after all, just texts themselves.[10] America becomes metaphor, the authors' "projection of an inner reality onto any external form that can bear and describe it" (Egan 19). America is both catalyst for and product of the autobiographical text; it is a cultural matrix as well as a geographical reality. The landscape Stein observes from an airplane merely frames her private America in *Everybody's Autobiography*; Hellman's ideal, politically ethical America does not exist in the 1970s in which she writes or in the 1950s' McCarthy era about which she writes; and Shepard's sense of place in *Motel Chronicles*, although grounded in the physical, sensual reality he experiences while traveling over the American landscape, often contradicts the mythical and spiritual experience he envisions as the American West. In the texts considered here, America becomes a secular system of belief that transcends mere geographical definition, and that secular system of belief supersedes the teleology of inheritance, family, genealogy, history, politics, and culture — the assumed context of identity formation in traditional autobiography.[11]

The United States, since its political inception, has been America the imagined, the idea, the dream, and those abstractions have accommodated and lured the infinitely diverse peoples who colonized the continent and displaced the native cultures and people. The texts discussed in this book evoke the feeling that America is evaporating as a concrete place. Like the first European transplants who defined themselves as Americans by breaking with Europe, Stein, Hellman, and Shepard continue an American autobiographical tradition visible in the work of Bradford, Franklin, Emerson, Whitman, Dickinson, Thoreau, and others. They alter the seemingly unalterable linear current of life and write a more real and ideal America, forging a new cultural and national identity for themselves. For all three writers, America remains an idea more than a system of government, a federation of states, or even a geographical location. For the first European transplants and for Stein, Hellman, and Shepard, the engendering of the autobiographical self intertwines with the rejection and rewriting of a centuries-old European collective identity.

Gertrude Stein's Everybody's Autobiography: The 1934-35 American Tour, a Landscape of Anxiety

Gertrude Stein had two Americas: the America she left in 1903 and internalized during the 31 years before she returned to it in 1934 and a real America (*EA* 192) whose tangible geographical features she exuberantly observed from an airplane. Stein's intense and long-standing contemplation of the nature and identity of America corresponds to her contemplation of her own identity in *Everybody's Autobiography*. Her public lecture tour of America resulted from her first commercial success, *The Autobiography of Alice B. Toklas* (1933); therefore, her re-encounter with America after thirty-one years of expatriation coincides with her becoming a celebrity, a commodity of the literary marketplace. The tour also encapsulates her traumatic confrontation with and subsequent resolution of the anxiety resulting from a split identity — between the writing, private self and the written, public self.

Everybody's Autobiography outlines a three-fold process of self-legitimization in which Stein asserts her powers of self-definition, first, by repudiating her origins and substituting those of her own invention; second, by equating herself with America in a reciprocal defining and engendering process; and last, by reconciling the split between her entity and identity. Stein becomes both the product and creator of America by replacing the usual organizing concepts of autobiography—human time and history and a developmental narrative structure of the human life span—with the paradigm of an America that both engenders and mirrors her genius, both "reflect[s] and determine[s] that self" (Kennedy, "Place" 497). She invents the autobiographical context composed of place and time: an America defined through a geography it transcends, and a continuous present that merges the time frames of composition and reading, or in other words, erases the boundary between the two activities.[1]

The key to unraveling Stein's contradictory view of self lies in the realization that she viewed entity as a permanent essence and identity as a series of fluctuating placeholders for the self. She explains the threatening split in identity she perceived in literary success:

> The thing is like this, it is all the question of identity. It is all a question of the outside being outside and the inside being inside. As long as the outside does not put a value on you it remains outside but when it does put a value on you then it gets inside or rather if the outside puts a value on you then all your inside gets to be outside [EA 47].

Identity is like an address that at one point can be "a name like your name" but can later be forgotten; identity is "something you do or do not remember" (EA 71) and is therefore not integral to the authentic writing self.[2] Stein envisions living as a vast and elusive process of trying to know yourself, but at the same time realizing that once you know, you are not "that thing": "The minute you or anybody else knows what you are you are not it, you are what you or anybody else knows you are" (EA 92). Identity, always one step ahead of knowledge, escapes it.

Understanding Stein's sense of self involves examining the complexities of her self-exile, which lasted from 1903 until her death in 1946. In choosing expatriation, Stein set a precedent for defining herself according to her presence or absence in a particular place; she thus disassociates self and origins.[3] This disassociation enables her simultaneously to acknowledge and reject her connection to America and her past. Thus, for all the importance that Stein attaches to the geographical features of a place and its influence on the human character and even physical appearance, she de-emphasizes the significance of physical presence in that place.[4]

The longest and most important chapter in *Everybody's Autobiography*, entitled "America," points to America's centrality in Stein's self-portrayal, but her statement regarding her arrival in New York with Alice Toklas indicates the degree to which she separates physical from mental place: "after all America is where we had been born and had always been even though for thirty years we had not really touched it with our feet and hands" (169). In *Everybody's Autobiography* she insists that "being there [in America] does not make me more there" (112), and implies that America is where she has been all along. Nor, she implies, does her being there or not being there call into question her status as "a good American" (301). She internalizes place, retroactively equates her long absence with presence, and creates the spatial equivalent of her continuous present. She lives the expatriate life while denying the actual physical exile of that life.

From the safe physical and emotional distance of her exile in France, Stein was able to bridge the discrepancy between her memory and the physical reality of America. But the psychological repercussions of her first visit to America in 31 years would challenge that ability. She would pronounce her childhood home, Oakland, California, no longer "there," and Cambridge, Massachusetts, where Stein did her undergraduate work at Radcliffe, completely "lost" to her memory. Those and other loose ends of memory that threaten Stein's seamless vision of an America nurtured in exile are banished and erased in 1935.

Everybody's Autobiography registers Stein's anxiety over a crisis of huge proportions: Am I the same me with public recognition as I am when "I write for myself and strangers" (*EA* 101)? Her deep-seated anxiety about origins and identity in general are apparent in her account of her own engendering. Speaking of "the fear of dying," she reveals the purely accidental nature of her existence: "anybody can think if I had died before there was anything but there is no thinking that one was never born until you hear accidentally that there were to be five children and if two little ones had not died there would be no Gertrude Stein, of course not" (115). Obviously, the possibility "that one was never born" haunted Stein.[5] Her contemplation of the fact that "there would be no Gertrude Stein" but for the unpredictable deaths of two of her siblings instilled in her a profound insecurity about the permanence and stability of herself. Recounting her family history in San Francisco, she again mentions the tenuousness of her existence: "two died in babyhood or else I would not have come nor my brother just two years older" (134). One might pinpoint Stein's acute awareness of her "replacement status" as the motivation to rewrite her origins. This act of self-legitimization could compensate for that sense of tenuous identity and her lifelong discomfort with it.

Inheriting her dead grandmother's *G* added to her feeling that she replaced a previously filled identity: "we were named after some one who is already dead, after all if they are living the name belongs to them so any one can be named after a dead one" (115).[6] Immediately following this explanation of how she was named, she reveals the anxiety she associates with knowing that she is a replacement both in body and name: "Identity always worries me and memory and eternity" (115).

To a great extent, she reconciles her anxiety over birth, death, identity, and entity by translating the threatening into the familiar. Thomas Couser notes the stabilizing effect the American tour and writing *Everybody's Autobiography* had on Stein: "In combination, perhaps, with her more private meditating and writing, the public acting out of the new role of celebrity and its recapitulation in *Everybody's Autobiography* seem to have restored Gertrude Stein to a sense of herself" ("Of Time" 803). Couser argues further that the ambiguous title, which implies that it is a text both of and for everybody, suggests that *Everybody's Autobiography* may be Stein's way of "recommend[ing] autobiography to everybody as a means of achieving self-confirmation, if not self-transcendence" ("Of Time" 803).

Everybody's Autobiography does record the American tour where Stein regained "a sense of herself," but it also reveals her considerable ambivalence and anxiety about returning to her native country. She repeatedly circles around her first monetary success, the publication of *The Autobiography of Alice B. Toklas*: "It is funny about money. And it is funny about identity. You are you because your little dog knows you, but when your public knows you and does not want to pay for you and when your public knows you and does want to pay for you, you are not the same you" (44–45). Her little dog's perspective, unaffected by literary success, provides Stein with a stable identity. Her audience's responses dictated Stein's level of confidence or anxiety. Stein concedes, "[Success] did change me" (47), and implies her helplessness in preventing that change: one cannot prevent the outside from "put[ting] a value on you" (47). Several critics have noted an unsureness of Stein's voice in *Everybody's Autobiography*, especially compared to the confident voice of *The Autobiography*, written several years earlier. Neil Schmitz characterizes the voice of *Everybody's Autobiography* as "troubled and uncertain" compared to "the magisterial 'I'" of *The Autobiography* (86).[7] Such readings emphasize the narrative or developmental aspects of the text; however, it is important to distinguish between the anxiety she experienced in America and recounts in her book from the anxiety she experienced in the writing act months later.

As early as her introduction, Stein mentions the anxiety evident in *Everybody's Autobiography*, and in this portion of the text she resolves the problem of identity before she formally explains it in the succeeding chapters. She encounters her photographic image in a shop window in New York and expresses pleasure with this instance of public recognition: "[M]y book Portraits and Prayers was just to come out that day and on the cover was to be a photograph of me by Carl Van Vechten and as we were walking down Fifth Avenue together, a young colored woman smiled and slowly pointed and there it was a copy of the book in a shop window and she smiled and went away" (8). Given her later anxious reactions to her name in lights at Times Square and to her image in the movie newsreels, in this retrospective moment of writing, Stein does not appear to feel the anxiety one would expect her to feel about yet another representation of self. However, in subsequent chapters about the American tour, she manufactures the appropriate vulnerability and anxiety. Stein retroactively creates and weaves the original anxiety into the text by writing in the psychological distance that places her concerns in a philosophical light. That she so pointedly re-creates the experience of anxiety indicates her effort to portray herself with psychological accuracy, even at the expense of her authoritative, confident public image or "magisterial" voice.

Stein repeatedly affirms how much she enjoys being a celebrity: "It was pleasant being a lion" (91). She had little trouble coping with the demands of public recognition. Rather, it was inexplicable observations that troubled her: "Everybody speaking to you everybody knowing you, everybody in a hotel or restaurant noticing you everybody asking you to write your name for them that was not the strangest thing. The strangest things were the streets, they were American streets, they really were, the people were American people but that was not such a difficult thing" (178). Evidently, Stein coped quite well with her popularity. The joy of public recognition and appreciation more than counterbalanced her anxiety. She embraces the American people; the "everybody" noticing her on the streets and in restaurants is "not the difficult thing." She does not struggle with the social aspects of her new public identity but with the consequences to her private self.

Stein's anxiety centers on scenes and places that overwhelmingly evoke in her a sense of "now" and "then"—of a division between past and present selves. These nodes of trauma rupture her map of memory and become points of erasure. Anxiety might be triggered by seeing her name in lights at Times Square, her film image in the movie newsreels, or memories of her student days in Cambridge, or her childhood home in Oakland. Each literal or figurative place is a site of trauma that she cannot easily assimilate into the seamless, categorized America she creates in the text. She encounters in America, according to Joseph Fichtelberg, "the Other she had evaded in France, the interminable multiplicity constituting the self" (195).

Particularly worrisome to Stein are her confrontations with visible signs that call attention to both the ephemeral nature of her identity and the threatening possibility of non-existence, even as they reaffirm her celebrity status. Her name in lights at Times Square and her screen image in a newsreel are tangible reminders that she does not completely own herself. Her name in lights disconcerts her: "[T]hen we saw an electric sign moving around a building and it said Gertrude Stein has come and that was upsetting" (175). Stein also had an unpleasant, "funny feeling" on seeing herself "almost as large and moving around and talking" on the movie screen (280). Her name or film image, like her "accidental" birth and her "inherited 'G,'" are placeholders conferred on her by chance or whim. Stein experiences both "shock[s] of recognition" and affirmation, and of "nonrecognition" as she glimpses the depths of non-existence, the potential erasure of self (175).

Stein's anxiety and ambivalence about her trip emerge most power-fully in the chapter "Preparations for going to America" and continue into the beginning of the "America" section, where she documents her rising doubts about visiting the physical place called America. Oddly enough, she envisions America as an approaching threat rather than as a static geo-graphical entity: "All this time America was coming nearer. Not that it had ever really been far away but it was certainly just now coming nearer that is to say it was getting more actual as a place where we might be" (111). America's "getting more actual" signals its rebirth for her as a phenome-non she cannot define or control.

The restrained account of her "preparations" and the retrospective exploration of the increasing anxiety she felt over the prospective tour are but controlling mechanisms, ways the text bridges gaps between the Stein for whom America was a comforting abstract and the Stein for whom America became an undeniable emotional reality. Stein's self-therapeutic prevarication in "Preparations for going to America" leads her (and the reader) to accept the tour as a reality: "[W]e knew that we were going to America and I was going to lecture" (163). She punctuates the end of the chapter with a decisive turnaround: "So we left for America" (165). With the next line, "We were going to America" (166), she opens the "America" chapter and re-emphasizes a decision that represents a revisiting of self as well as a revisiting of place.

Her initial resistance to going on tour, coupled with her gradual acceptance of America as a physical place, signals Stein's need to control the inevitable, and in some cases troubling, upsurge of memories associ-ated with reconnecting the exiled self and the homeland. When her agent, Mr. Bradley, first suggested that she go on the lecture tour, she strongly resisted the idea: "I said I would not go to America" (124). Her equivoca-tion reaches a crisis in *Everybody's Autobiography* when, within a four-line span, she makes a decision and then dramatically reverses it: "[A]nd so we decided not to go to America" becomes "[A]nd then we did go to America" (132). The confrontation and reconciliation of these private and public selves, represented by resistance and acceptance, become the central drama in the text.

Stein experiences anxiety over intangible as well as visible representations of herself. The anticipation of speaking in public before a very large audience for the first time provokes a severe anxiety attack that temporarily incapacitates her. Stein loses her voice upon learning that, despite her expressed wishes never to lecture to an audience of more than five hundred, she was to lecture to more than a thousand people at Columbia University. Ulla Dydo cites a precedent for this anxious reaction to lecturing in 1934. Upon her "first invitation [extended by Edith Sitwell] to speak before a live audience," the Literary Society at Cambridge, England, in 1926, "Stein ... panicked and at first declined" ("Landscape" 97). The nature of Stein's anxiety on this occasion is relevant to her reaction to lecturing in America: "She must have sensed as soon as she received the invitation that the temptation to please an audience would interfere with composition and that a live audience would make her personality rather than her words the focus of attention. The prospect left her anxious precisely because it was seductive" ("Landscape" 99).

Lecturing at first seemed a great compromise of identity. Stein feared the result of language's becoming a primarily aural rather than visual experience. When talking, one ceases to be inside oneself and instead hears what others hear one say. Having to filter listening through the reactions of other people obliterates the purity, the first-hand, visual experience of language. One's own words are mediated, distorted, and stolen by the interpreting listener. For Stein, writing and talking are two separate activities — "the two are not one" (264).

Stein avoids dealing with the dramatic implications of losing her voice by evasively attributing it to general properties she has assigned to America's air and food: "I was not accustomed to heated apartments, we heat very sparingly in Paris and besides Paris is moist, the food is dry and the air is moist and in New York the food was moist and the air was dry, so gradually I was certain that there was something the matter with my throat and I would not be able to speak anywhere" (176–77). Bolstered by "the nice doctor we had met on the Champlain [the ship on which she and Toklas crossed the Atlantic]" (177), Stein triumphantly regained her voice, lectured at Columbia, and lost her fear of public speaking: "after the first [lecture] I never was [afraid] again. Not at all" (177).

To avoid the inevitable divisions caused by time and history, Stein consistently denies that the America she left in 1903 and the one she finds in 1934 differ. Her need to rediscover or confirm her private vision of the America she had lived with overrules her need to discover a new one. Logically speaking, however, the country she was to visit could not possibly correspond to the privately constructed America she had lived with for thirty-one years. Joseph Fichtelberg calls her experience of an "unchanged" America a "liberation" (however contrived it must have been): "Stein could declare her country unchanged, even after a war, a crash, and a depression" (194). She knits the two Americas together as she denies their differences. Stein believed that countries, like people, "have to be what they are" (235). She reiterates her belief in America's unchangeable nature in the close of *Wars I Have Seen*, her effusive tribute to the America that liberated France: "When I was in America in '34 they asked me if I did not find Americans changed. I said no what could they change to, just to become more American. No I said I could have gone to school with any of them" (259). Her assertion that nations, like herself, have basic, unchangeable character traits enables her to comfortably use America in the equation establishing equilibrium between the "I" and the "not-I," between herself and the strange new America she encounters.

She conflates past and present to eradicate the disturbing differences between the new-found and the remembered America: "When they used to ask me in America whether I had not found America changed I said no of course it had not changed what could it change to" (69–70). She assures us that America "looks just as you expect it to look but it does not look real" (171). Even travel conditions have changed little: "They use words like air-conditioned but it smells just about the same" (166). Even cities gradually come to resemble Stein's 30-year-old memories of them. Chicago, at first unfamiliar, "came to be more the one I can remember" (193). A California left in 1892 becomes "our California" (294) or "our country" (198), both acquiring new identities that gloss over differences between the past and present. On the train ride to Baltimore, "where all [Stein's] people come from," she "knew the name of everything and the woods looked as [she] remembered them they did" (230). She finds decidedly different "the [American] roads and what is on them"; however, "the rest is as it was" (293). Paradoxically, whatever in America is different is also the same.[8]

Peculiar exceptions to Stein's inability to bridge past and present are her experiences at Cambridge, Massachusetts, and Oakland, California. These locations evoke reactions similar to but stronger than those evoked by representations of herself, perhaps because they force Stein to re-encounter selves of decades before: "It was funny about Cambridge it was the one place where there was nothing that I recognized nothing…. [T]hat day Cambridge was so different that it was as if I had never been there there was nothing there that had any relation to any place that had been there. I lost Cambridge then and there.... That is funny" (187). Stein lived in Cambridge from 1894 to 1897. One can only speculate on the motive for repressing the memories of her years there. Here she encounters a breach in memory that echoes her anxiety over her chance birth — the realization that had two other siblings not died, she would be nonexistent. This anxiety suggests a repressed trauma:[9] "[I]t was as if I had never been there."

Oakland, too, becomes an absence: "[I]t was not natural to have come from [Oakland].... [T]here is no there there" (289). The Cambridge remembered, the one intact and "there" in memory, no longer exists when she visits it; it is "nothing." The identities and realities of Cambridge and Oakland as places become absences, just names with "no there there." Stein's return to Oakland is a "simulacrum of a larger textual crisis" that exposes her to the plurality of the self (Fichtelberg 195). However, unlike Shepard, who embraces a galaxy of selves, she tenaciously resists the insistent memories that threaten to splinter a unified sense of self. The adult Stein who now encounters Oakland and Cambridge has given birth to herself as a twentieth-century literary genius and can therefore diminish the importance of childhood and adolescent memories in her current vision of the self as a twentieth-century genius and literary celebrity.[10]

Extrapolating from her ability to deny the existence of places once significant to her, she also denies the existence of people once significant to her. There is a significant parallel to Stein's reactions to the disappearance of these two locations from her landscape of memory: her reaction to her break with her older brother Leo, a close companion from her childhood into early adulthood, once Alice B. Toklas superseded him in importance. Like Oakland and Cambridge, he becomes an absence and silence in her emotional landscape despite the fact that he had once been integral to Stein's existence: "But [Leo's jealousy] destroyed him for me and it destroyed me for him" (77). She effectively proclaims Leo to be no longer "there": "Little by little we never met again" (77).

The Autobiographer as "Everybody"

Stein's sweeping statement in her introduction to *Everybody's Autobiography*, "Anything is an autobiography" (5), authoritatively cancels traditional definitions of autobiography and indicates Stein's indifference to genre boundaries. This autobiographical work extends to an extreme degree the egocentric individualism of the nineteenth century, for the self is both the origin and the literary product of the text. An eclectic collection of genres, *Everybody's Autobiography* includes miniature philosophical treatises on identity and her work with William James at Radcliffe, art history and the artist's duty to art, and commentary on politics and her absolutely negative view on government ("[T]here is no reason for it" [153]). *Everybody's Autobiography* pointedly warns the reader that the text constitutes a philosophical quest as much as it constitutes autobiography.

Seemingly in self-contradiction, however, she is also intent on establishing the generic division between autobiography and novels: "Any autobiography is not a novel no indeed it is not a novel" (194). According to Stein, autobiography in the twentieth century has supplanted novels, publicity and the media have usurped fiction's domain, and genre divisions have collapsed. In her 1935 lecture on narration, Stein ponders the changing definitions of narrative and the difficulty of distinguishing it from non-narrative. She concurs with Hellman's definition of autobiography as adherence to a strict chronology: "There are now several questions is there anything that is not narrative and what is narrative what has narrative gotten to be now. When one used to think of narrative one meant a telling of what is happening in successive moments of its happening. ... But now we have changed all that we really have. We really now do not really know that anything is progressively happening" (*Narration* 17).[11] Acknowledging the death of the novel, she advises young writers to write essays, "since characters are of no importance" (102). Characters require identity, and eliminating the character element in writing circumvents the problem of identity. Publicity and autobiography also render the novelist's imagination unnecessary: the Duchess of Windsor, for example, was "a more real person to the public and while the divorce was going on was a more actual person than anyone could create" (*TI* 22).

Stein explains how the public's ability to construct hyper-real (i.e., actual) identity undermines the novelist's belief in her work:

> In the old days when they wrote novels they made up the personality of the things they had seen in people and the things that were the people as if they were a dream. But now well now how can you dream about a personality when it is always being created for you by a publicity, how can you believe what you make up when publicity makes them up to be so much realer than you can dream. And so autobiography is written which is in a way a way to say that publicity is right, they are as the public sees them. Well yes [69].

Her questions How can you dream? and How can you believe? reveal the doubts that haunt her and interfere with her efforts to write. Autobiography and biography, types of hyper-realism for Stein, replace fiction. The power of publicity to make people "so much realer" can, she insists, destroy "what you make up"— can even render it superfluous. Stein envisions the media as an insidious threat not only to her financial success, but to her confidence in her identity as a writer.

Her most dreaded speculation is that public identity is "right," that, indeed, being defined by one's audience can result in the loss of an "inside," private identity. That publicity is "right" affirms the audience's view of the writer's personality over the writer's authentic self as experienced subjectively. The writing self of the autobiography that "is written" (i.e., "identity") is "as the public sees [it]," not as the writing self (i.e., "entity") experiences it. She tacitly acknowledges the overwhelming power of publicity over the individual's sense of self. Her questions, which suggest the increasing difficulty of dreaming or believing, of preserving the imagination as a relevant and viable component of writing, mirror her central dilemma: how to remain the agent of one's own literary work in a world increasingly intent on manufacturing identities to feed public demand. Thus, Stein acknowledges the futility of capturing the self even as she writes a text ostensibly dedicated to doing just that. *Everybody's Autobiography* is an ingenious textual compromise in which the opposing demands of two types of autobiographical discourse meet: the introverted, confessional mode focusing on the author's need to portray the self to the self, and the more public form, the memoir portraying the self in relation to others.

Stein, like many twentieth-century autobiographers, designs an autobiographical model that rejects the time-bound traditional ones. Memory and individual time are no longer the "primary organising principle[s] of experience" (Russo 39–40). Reliance on memory and individual time has produced the traditional experiential categories that make up autobiography, each of which adopts a narrative model: the conversion narrative, the Eden narrative, the confession, the journey narrative, the memoir, and others. However, replacement models must be invented for Augustine's God's time, for Henry James's individual time, and for Malraux's historical time, for example (Russo 40).

For Stein, the paradigm of America replaces human or religious time, and serves as an achronological organizational concept that permits the overlap and superimposition of various time frames and selves. The chapter titles delineate a journey narrative. An example of this technique is found in the introduction, which conflates the writing moment and the recent past and playfully ruptures the text's "retrospective" time frame:

"The other day this is March nineteen thirty-six my brother in California that is another story a rather nice story" (*EA* 11). Here, the moment of writing and the story from "the other day" weave like stray strands through the text, rendering impossible a closed time frame and creating the continuous present. Frequently used phrases such as "day before yesterday" and "just today" (210) diminish the text's historical authority. Distracting promises, such as "but that is a later story" (14), "I will tell later all about" (15) and "We will all see him [Picabia] again" (17), destroy the narrative suspense. They also dash any expectations we might have that Stein's text recounts the events of her life in the sequence they occurred.[12]

Conflating the role of author and critic, she validates her personal definition of autobiography and situates *Everybody's Autobiography* in her own canon, measuring its success in relation to two other "autobiographical narratives"—*The Making of Americans* and *The Autobiography of Alice B. Toklas*. She admits that *The Making of Americans* "is not really a story it is a description" (133), and characterizes *The Autobiography* as mere newspaper writing or illustration, "a description and a creation of something that having happened was in a way happening not again" (302). Pleased with *Everybody's Autobiography*, Stein announces near the end of the book, "And now in this book I have done it if I have done it" (303). She had achieved the type of narrative she thought worthy of a genius: "a simple narrative of what is happening not as if it had happened not as if it is happening but as if it is existing simply that thing" (303). Years later, Stein re-evaluated her high opinion of the text. She comments in her 1946 "Transatlantic Interview": "I think *Paris France* and *Wars I Have Seen* are the most successful of this [the subject of narration]. I thought I had done it in *Everybody's Autobiography*. I worked very hard on that and was often very exhausted, but it is often confused and not clarified. But in *Wars I Have Seen* and in *Paris France*, to my feeling, I have done it more completely" (19).

For Stein, the narrative act serves as both experiential model and subject of the text. The brief introduction stands separately as a summary, an affirmation and encapsulation of the book.[13] Thus, it undermines and mimics the ostensible purpose of autobiography and dismantles any chronological order (based on the American tour) the reader may be tempted to impose on the book. The introduction reveals a preoccupation with the production of autobiography and is unconstrained by the linear narrative progression promised by the chapter headings: "What happened after The Autobiography of Alice B. Toklas," "What was the effect upon me of the Autobiography," "Preparations for going to America," "America," and "Back again."

On the first page of the text, Stein's non sequitur about writing auto-biography both acknowledges and ignores her generic intentions: "This is the way any autobiography has to be written which reminds me of Dashiell Hammett. But before I am reminded of Dashiell Hammett I want to say that just today I met Miss Hennessy" (3). She immediately dismisses any expectations the reader may have for an orderly story and objectifies her own mental processes, for clearly she is already reminded of Hammett even as she defers being reminded of him. It is nearly 300 pages later before the text returns, as promised ("when the dinner happens later" [5]), to the anecdote about the dinner party with Dashiell Hammett in Hollywood. With Shandean organization, she delays beginning the book: "Being pho-tographed together reminds me of another thing and then chapter one will begin" (6). Such an unconventional and manipulative introduction con-tradicts the title's promise and reveals her agenda: defining what she does in the process of doing it, analyzing the genre as much as she examines the events of her life.

The first two chapters of *Everybody's Autobiography*, constituting one third of the book and entitled "What happened after The Autobiography of Alice B. Toklas" and "What was the effect upon me of the Autobiogra-phy," establish *The Autobiography* as a base upon which *Everybody's Auto-biography* is constructed. Chapter 1 summarizes the birth of *The Autobi-ography*, thereby enfolding the gestation of that text into the beginning of *Everybody's Autobiography*. The first two chapters also emphasize that prior text's role in evoking the present one and point to its role in providing narrative continuity between Stein's two autobiographical ventures: "If there had not been a beautiful and unusually dry October at Bilignin in France in nineteen thirty two followed by an unusually dry and beautiful first two weeks of November would The Autobiography of Alice B. Tok-las have been written. Possibly but probably not then" (9). Stein's specu-lation about whether *The Autobiography* would have been written had cer-tain conditions not existed recapitulates her birth anxiety, which she projects onto the engendering of her autobiographical text: "[T]here were to be five children and if two little ones had not died there would be not Gertrude Stein" (115).

Despite the unconventional method in the book's introduction, Stein transforms two orthodox characteristics of traditional autobiography in this anti-autobiographical text, two characteristics used much more con-ventionally by Hellman in *Scoundrel Time*, for example. Both authors exhibit a prophetic attitude toward the reading public and a quest for self-knowledge. Prophetic autobiography is an American mode of memoir that derives from "the Puritan belief in the redemptive power of individual

effort." It is "a way of narrating true experience" to a "community working toward an ideal nation" (Waterson on Couser 193).

William Spengemann and L. R. Lundquist's view of the genre as
"an instrument of knowledge" (501) combines the collective and egocentric motives involved in writing autobiography, and thus accommodates
Stein's self-centered purposes. Their first category is prophets, "restless
types searching for truth, undergoing personal metamorphosis, interpreting the holy mysteries of their tribe, [and] forecasting the collective
destiny" (509).[14] As a secular version of a prophet, Stein searches for the
truth about the self's relationship to the self, and the "holy mysteries"
she ponders are the secrets of what it means to be American. Her tone
sometimes resembles that of a prophet or teacher on a sojourn, a hero
who acquires knowledge in another land and presents it to the community.

Stein achieves the self-transcendence associated with prophetic autobiography—"the ability to exist beyond the self and beyond time"—in a
purely secular sense (Couser, "Of Time" 787, 795). Thomas Couser draws
parallels between Jonathan Edwards, Thoreau, and Stein by emphasizing
their departure from the purely religious perspective characteristic of the
original Puritan model of prophetic autobiography. In a description that
also summarizes Hellman's role in *Scoundrel Time*, Elizabeth Waterson
describes Stein's and Thoreau's translation of the prophetic role into secular terms: they are both prophets in the "Old Testament sense of hold-
ing a supramundane view, feeling a compulsion to recount personal experience as significant ... imagining an audience who may be wandering in
the wilderness, chosen for a special destiny" (194). Stein's America comprises that "wandering" audience that must be led to its "special destiny"—
an appreciation of her work. *Everybody's Autobiography* is her "dialogue
with America en masse" (Couser, "Of Time" 801–02) in which she speaks
in college lecture halls, confronts the media, and wanders the streets of
American cities. Stein confronts the anathema of her identity crisis and
makes peace with herself.

In this "collective dialogue," Stein generalizes about Americans as a
group, rather than as a collection of individually portrayed personalities.
This enables her to define "the American" as an absolute and establish
that term as one by which she subsequently defines herself. The text is
the "Autobiography of every one" (99)—and, she implies, is *for* everyone—but she need not, as she did in *The Making of Americans* (1906–08),
go through the lengthy process of describing each "one" individually.
Everybody's Autobiography includes, under the generic identity of "everybody," the infinite variety of Americans she strove to portray in *The*

Making of Americans: "Everybody speaking to you everybody knowing you, everybody in a hotel or restaurant noticing you everybody asking you to write your name for them" (178). The repeated "everybody" Stein confronts as a recognized celebrity is clearly her American public, a public sometimes named specifically — photographers, reporters, old friends, American celebrities such as Mary Pickford and Dashiell Hammett — and sometimes incorporated under the generic "everybody."

Stein stands in for each person who "is or was or shall be living" (99) — that is, she assumes the collective identity of "everybody" — and focuses on the relation of the self to the self. *Everybody's Autobiography* need not reveal "any connection between any one and any one because now there is none" (99). In the progression from *The Making of Americans*, to *The Autobiography*, to *Everybody's Autobiography*, she shifts her focus from the publicly defined self to the self-defined self. The change demonstrates her philosophy as expressed to Robert Maynard Hutchins and Mortimer Adler (originators of the Great Books program) at the University of Chicago: "[T]he real ideas are not the relation of human beings as groups but a human being to himself inside him" (206).

Stein's portrait of "everybody" derives from her quasi-scientific observations and conclusions, and it threatens to overshadow her own self-portrait in *Everybody's Autobiography*. The subjects of the numerous, concise biographies she inserts into the text range in importance from Picabia, whom Stein considered "too brilliant" (57), to people whose names she herself does not know or has forgotten. She explains her disregard for the importance of names: "I used to think the name of anybody was very important and the name makes you and I have often said so ... but still there are so many names and anybody nowadays can call anybody any name they like" (10). Her diminishing belief in the importance of names and the public identity attached to them suggests a possible explanation for the title of *Everybody's Autobiography*, a text which, by definition, requires a proper name in its title. The substitution of the pronoun *everybody* for a proper name both rejects and includes all names. Her identification with all Americans blurs the distinction between self-portraiture and biography and rejects the unified self implied by the singular, first-person pronoun: "[T]his is to be everybody's autobiography" (6). In addition, her pronounced indifference to names recalls her discomfort with her dead grandmother's *G*; to escape proper names is to escape the identity she inherited through a relative's death and to reaffirm her control over defining herself.

Stein acknowledges the unified self as a fiction. But her expressed suspicion about the principles of autobiography and traditional narrative creates a tension between what she is actually *doing*—writing autobiography—and what she professes to believe is possible.

> And identity is funny being yourself is funny as you are never yourself to yourself except as you remember yourself and then of course you do not believe yourself. That is really the trouble with an autobiography you do not of course you do not really believe yourself why should you, you know so well so very well that it is not yourself, it could not be yourself because you cannot remember right. ... You are of course never yourself [68].

Autobiography is futile, for one can never establish a neutral space from which to observe objectively the self in order to convey it textually to others. The self one remembers is never the self who recalls it. Her obliquely autobiographical or biographical titles, *The Making of Americans*, *The Autobiography of Alice B. Toklas*, and *Everybody's Autobiography*, resist naming herself, but nevertheless refer to the self and tacitly promise a textual version of that self. Her rejection of the mainstays of the autobiographical tradition, as summarized by Paul Jay—"to transcend, to restore, and to reconcile" a pre-existing, unified self—implies her recognition of the self as "shattered, scattered, decentered" ("Being" 1056), and therefore fictional.

Stein's self-contradictions complicate her concept of the self, whether unified or fragmented, multiple or singular. At times she views herself as a series of identities that are as easily forgotten as are addresses, and at other times as an unchangeable entity, a core self similar to Hellman's—based on "character" and impervious to influences of time, history, and public recognition. Her comment on General Grant alludes to the unchangeable core of the self (and complements the belief that nations, too, have unchangeable natures): "[A]nd after all what can anybody change to, they have to be what they are and they are" (*EA* 235). In this statement she argues, as Hellman did until her last works, for the integrity of the self, for an eternal essence that anchors identity.

On the other hand, Stein's view that identity is like an address, a product of memory and therefore forgettable and dispensable, "denies the resemblance between her past and present 'selves' which lies behind 'functional' identity" (Neuman, "Gertrude Stein's Dog" 63, n. 3). Stein's acceptance of functional identity as serial and fragmented implies that those identities do not necessarily share a set of common memories or derive from the same core being. Viewing the self as a series of identities requires the separation of the writing and written selves; a distinction must be made between the "I" who speaks or writes and the "I" who is spoken, between the subject and object of the text.

The narrative voice's easy, pervasive fluctuation between "I" and "we" appears on the first page of *Everybody's Autobiography* and establishes simultaneous individual and collective identities.[15] We easily assume that here "we" means Stein and Toklas: "[A]nd anyway I did write The Autobiography of Alice B. Toklas and since then a great many things happened, and the first thing that happened was that we came back to Paris, we generally almost always do do that" (9–10). Instead, "we" is a placeholder that, depending on the context, may refer to Stein and Alice Toklas, or to an ambiguous collective identity. Statements such as "Anyway we went out to San Leandro where we used to ride on a tandem bicycle in the dust" (*EA* 291) and "Saint Helena is where we used to take the stage coach" (*EA* 293) are particularly confusing. Although Stein reminisces about California—which is also Alice Toklas's home state—the "we" does not refer to Alice because she and Alice were not childhood friends. She may covertly refer to Leo, whose name she avoids mentioning in her texts, usually referring to him instead as "my brother." We are left to speculate.

Stein exploits the paradoxical nature of identity—the fact that it means both "sameness and distinctiveness," both relation to others and relation to the self (Gardiner 347). Philippe Lejeune comments on the power of alternating pronouns to express the multiplicity of identity enclosed within the myth of the self, a model that epitomizes Shepard's sense of plural identity[16]:

> [A] system of oscillation and indecision allows the writer to avoid the artificial incompleteness of ["I" and "he"]. If "I" and "he" reciprocally eclipse one another, is it not best to use each alternately for the unmasking of one by the other?... This plan [alternating pronouns] ... obviously corresponds to contemporary anxieties and, sometimes, to reflections on modern theories of personality [39].

The two personas of *Everybody's Autobiography*, "I" and "we," interpenetrate and are typically evasive, quirky, and ambiguous.[17] The reciprocal eclipse indefinitely defers the arrival at a unified identity by creating a multi-voiced subject. Stein's text exhibits what Sidonie Smith calls the "complex double-voicedness" and the "fragile heteroglossia" often found in women's autobiography (*Poetics* 50). According to Philippe Lejeune, no combination of personal pronouns can "fully express" the autobiographer: "All imaginable combinations reveal ... the nature of the person—the tension between impossible unity and intolerable division and the fundamental schism which turns the speaker into a fugitive" (32). "I" simultaneously represents Stein the generic American and the "everybody" of her title. "We" encompasses not only her personal relationship with Alice Toklas, but the voice of the American people whom she represents.

Geography, Memory, and America

On her American tour, Stein ventures into unknown aspects of herself and her native country, converts the unknown into the familiar, and assembles her past into a seamless context. She assimilates and absorbs America, converting its people, characteristics, geography, and history into parts of herself. "Preparations for going to America," "America," and "Back again" establish America as Stein's extra-textual reference point for the last two thirds of *Everybody's Autobiography*. The chapter title "America" signals a shift in focus: America is not only a geographical reality; it is an idea. But the title of the last chapter, "Back again," implies that America never replaced Paris as the internal reference point for her writing self.

This process of conversion and reinterpretation of things American insures that her text and the self she creates are defined in relation to her, not in relation to a pre-determined, collective definition of America. America becomes a familial substitute, assuming the functions of various hereditary factors and emotional influences. She projects her anxieties onto America's landscape and systematically objectifies and conquers them. In explaining this phenomenon, J. Gerald Kennedy writes, "Place often operates as a mirror [for the self], allowing the writer to represent identifying qualities through a putatively external scene" ("Place" 497). Her revision of current and family history as she reinterprets America and invents the self stems from her obsessions about the possibility of never being born and the inheritance of her dead grandmother's *G*.

But Stein's attempts to subsume objective reality and transform it into her subjective reality often over-simplify history by conflating major historical events with her everyday impressions. History filtered through her experience becomes secondary to her personal narrative, and she circumvents the autobiographical necessity of placing herself in the context of human history. Rather, human history *places itself in the context of Stein*. More than any other strategy in Stein's autobiographical method, this solipsism reveals the extent of her egotism and her insecurity about identity. And no other technique so clearly argues for her deliberate rejection of political and cultural assumptions underlying the patriarchal project of history.

Unlike traditional autobiographers who acknowledge the primary narrative of history and current events, narratives simultaneously independent and inclusive of all narratives, she addresses the war in Europe, for example, only as it affects her everyday life.[18] She mentions the economic depression in America in passing: "[T]hey built this university [Duke] and now there was the depression and they did not have very much money" (*EA* 252). A reference to the Spanish Civil War — "And now this is Bilignin and now this is the Spanish revolution" (131) — merely sets the stage for her personal narrative.

She subordinates her hints about the sinister political climate of the 1930s to the narrative about her regular walks in Paris with her dog Basket: "[T]here began to be on all the walls political posters and everybody instead of commencing began to stop and silently read them.... So I took Basket and I stood and read everything" (95–96). Her account of the numerous comments and questions Basket evokes from people in the street (regarding his breed, how often he is bathed, how "sweet" he is) dominates her description of the nightly gatherings in the street: "Gradually more people were getting together and every evening at the corner of the boulevard Raspail and the boulevard Saint Germain they were gathering and every evening more and more were gathering" (96). She mentions seeing men with bandages and being told "that they had been at the Place de la Concorde and everybody had been fired upon and that was the beginning" (98).[19] But she fails to follow up on this thought-provoking introduction, saying, "It was not the beginning nothing more was happening" (98). History and politics, here, threaten to break out of their subordinate, incidental role of highlighting her evening walks with Basket; therefore, her next comment, "There was no connection between anything happening this winter" (98), signals her choice to use as autobiographical material only historical events that enhance the story of her own life.

Stein's famous statement about her father's death in her childhood, "Then our life without a father began a very pleasant one" (142), by logical extension equates her personal opinion with universal human experience:

> There is too much fathering going on just now and there is no doubt about it fathers are depressing. Everybody nowadays is a father, there is father Mussolini and father Hitler and father Roosevelt and father Stalin and father Lewis and father Blum and father Franco is just commencing now and there are ever so many more ready to be one. Fathers are depressing [133].[20]

If autobiography is, as Sidonie Smith states, "ultimately an assertion of arrival and embeddedness in the phallic order" (*Poetics* 40), Stein's multivocal text openly confronts and denies that destination and converts historical events into mere examples of patriarchal oppression. Her concentration on her own reactions — "Fathers are depressing" — overrides the importance of the major historical events to which she alludes. Her egotistical focus on the personal perspective decenters the patriarchal narrative of history and establishes her own experience as the legitimate historical context.

Even when generalizing about human nature, Stein repeatedly reinforces the dominance of individual tendencies and preferences over collective ones. However, in characteristic self-contradiction, she also more than once mentions her habit of asking even total strangers "the name and occupation and what their father did and where they were born" (203–04). In *Wars I Have Seen*, she explains her interest in the states of origin and the occupations of American soldiers stationed in Europe during World War II:

> What we always wanted to know was the state they came from and what they did before they came over here.... [B]ut what we wanted most was to hear them say the name of the state in which they were born and the names of the other states where they had lived.... [T]he thing I like most are the names of all the states of the United States. They make music and they are poetry [249].

This interest in the particulars of each soldier reveals the contradiction between her theories and her practical beliefs about what shapes people. Like Hellman, she ultimately retained a paradoxical essentialism, and was unconventional only in that she defined the terminology of that essentialism with comforting generalizations about the American character.

Stein recalls a statement made by a member of the Sûreté, the French Police, when she and Alice Toklas were preparing their legal papers for their participation in the war effort. His comment introduces her concise biography of her family lineage extending to her maternal grandfather born in 1800:

> He came to see us and we went into the matter of where we were born and where our parents were born and where our grandparents were born and then he said and what is the difference any way. Nowadays nobody really is going to feel one way because their father or their mother certainly not their grandfather or their grandmother were born in one country rather than another [230].

Here Stein co-opts the official's opinion about the insignificance of family history to introduce a summary of her genealogy. She allows the reader to assume that she too believes in the irrelevance of national origin by silently endorsing the policeman's view and folding it into her own. Individual character, she implies, dominates cultural, social, and nationalistic factors. Thus, the individual decides how she "is going to feel." The ambiguous "nobody" and "their" incorporate an alternative interpretation: people in general no longer consider national or cultural origins as significant in forming opinions about other people.

Even the significance of individual family members is overshadowed by their roles in Stein's existence. Stein neatly reinterprets, pastes in and glosses over the material of her past to augment and buttress the moment of writing. She avoids the specifics of personality about "aunt Fanny" and "uncle Eph" (231) until she brings her narrative out of the historic-genealogical digression and it once again intersects with the time frame of the American tour. The text makes the transition from the historical past tense to the present tense of the narrative: "This time I did not see my relations" (231). Her repugnance for family — the desire "to escape this philosophically and psychologically unhealthy circuit of melodramatic remembering and forgetting" (Parke 561) — precludes the writing of a family history in the conventional sense. The introduction of her family relations by name relegates them to points on the map of her tour. Aunt Fanny and Uncle Eph merely designate where she did *not* go and what she did *not* do.

Because Stein values relation of the self to the self more than she values the relation of the self to others, she rejects family as integral to individual identity. Instead, Stein retroactively defines her family history as she defines herself, in terms of geographical place: "[A]fter all America is where we had been born and had always been" (*EA* 169). As Catherine Parke explains, the family epitomizes identity as relation to others, "legislates cause-and-effect thinking and deprives us of the present" (563). Family, as a network of individuals defined through their relatedness to one another, takes on the tyrannical function of any historical narrative and becomes "the formal codification of memory" (Parke 563). As members of a family, we can know ourselves only second-hand through others, not from direct experience with the self:

> Well anyway my grandfather my mother's father was not born in Baltimore but he was born very long ago he was born in 1800 so I have been told and before he was twenty he had come to Baltimore and after that he was always there. ... My father's family did not come there as soon they came just before the civil war, and they wandered they were not always there, and they were not all of them there, a number of them but not all of them as my mother's family had been and so my

> mother's family who were people who were always there did not con-
> sider my father's family as quite equal to them [*EA* 230–31].

She refers to her father's and mother's families generically — "my father's family" and "my mother's family" (231) — and diminishes their social status and prejudices to a matter of place. Stein reduces her mother's side of the family to people who were "always there" and her father's family to people who "wandered" and "were not always there." She describes both sides of her family in terms of general tendencies; they operate not as individuals but almost as migrating landmarks on the American landscape that inexplicably relocate over time.

In *Everybody's Autobiography*, Stein eliminates both parental sources of nurturing and influence and makes their absences invisible and un-traumatic by replacing them with a history that writes them out and renders them insignificant. She omits from her discussion of her family the unquestioned and all-embracing affection she has for America and Americans. She tersely dismisses her mother, saying that because "she had been ill a long time and had not been able to move around," when she died everyone "already had the habit of doing without her" (138).[21] Stein reaffirms her independent, self-defined status by duplicating in her text her mother's virtual absence in real life. One might sum up her attitude toward her parents by noting the absence of mothering, "too much fathering," followed by a "pleasant time" after her father's death. For Stein, mothering is a more benign activity; it is not "cheering," but mothers are "not as depressing as fathers" (133). Clearly, the narrative of her rise to genius and her influence on twentieth-century art subsumes what she considers minor narratives pertaining to siblings, parents, and cultural origins.

It is to the much earlier autobiographical text, *The Making of Americans*, that Stein had relegated the issues of family entanglements, and she refers the readers of *Everybody's Autobiography* to it for further details on her family: "[I]n the beginning I did give a real description of how our family lived in East Oakland, and how everything looked as I had seen it then" (69). *The Making of Americans* is Stein's attempt to create "a history of every individual person who ever is or was or shall be living" (*EA* 99). The text's repetition and incremental variation methodically explore all the possible permutations of the human personality, "every one, every one who could or would or had been living" (*EA* 69). Joseph Fichtelberg defines one third of that text as "concealed autobiography," and cites "her observations of Baltimore cousins" as the source for most of the rest of the text (171). However, by the writing of *Everybody's Autobiography* in 1937, her focus had shifted from the particular to the general, from her family and origins to self-legitimization.

Self-Legitimization: The Basis for the Autobiographical Self

When Paul John Eakin aptly says that F. Scott Fitzgerald's "Crack-Up" essays reflect "an interdependency" and "intense identification between his own life and the life of his time" (*Fictions* 207), he identifies a phenomenon often attributed to canonical American autobiographers such as Whitman, Thoreau, and Henry Adams — a phenomenon certainly discernible in Hellman and Shepard as well. However, Stein's fixation on defining America goes beyond an identification with it. Like Fitzgerald, and Hellman, she also envisioned herself as a "representative individual" (*Fictions* 207), but in *Everybody's Autobiography*, she reveals personal motives that surpass the need to speak prophetically to the collective. Those motives include more than merely doing what G. Thomas Couser calls "defin[ing] her genius in relation to the development of her nation and its need for a spokesman" ("Of Time" 801). Even her democratic impulses for the good of collective America are ruled by very self-centered motives.

The self Stein constructs in *Everybody's Autobiography* relies on her personalized and interdependent concepts of Americanism and genius. She implies that America's landscape can be read and interpreted like a text, but only by an American genius. She interprets the aerial view of the landscape as "post-cubist" (191) and thus confirms the avant-garde roots from which she springs.[22] The "America" chapter draws general conclusions about America's landscape, the American people, and patriotism, and presents them as indisputable truths.

For Stein, Americanism had little to do with an attachment to the geographical reality of place. Thus, her individualistic views on Americanism and expatriation brought her to a paradoxical position on "the relation between place and self" (Kennedy, "Place" 516). However violated or split Stein's private self may have been by the intruding, adoring public, she was unshakable in her Americanism: "I am an American all right" (*EA* 112) and "I am a good American" (*EA* 301). The years of World War II only intensified her Americanism. In *Wars I Have Seen*, she contends that "naturalisation is foolishness completely" (131) and announces the impossibility of anyone's ever shaking off or replacing one's connection to the birth nation with a devotion to and understanding of another chosen country:

> Nobody not born in a country or if they are born in another country
> by accident must be born of parents born in that country, nobody not
> born in a country has really the ultimate feeling of that country. Let
> them have all the privileges of residence, of earning their living in that
> country or of enjoying that country but not of becoming citizens of
> that country. Citizenship is a right of birth and should remain so....
> [O]ne's native land is one's native land you cannot get away from it
> [131–32].

Here Stein parallels Lillian Hellman, who also falls back on her Americanism in trying to explain inexplicable tendencies and justify her moral judgments. Also, she again adopts an essentialism modeled on what she has chosen to do as a long-term expatriate in France. Writing shortly before her death in 1946, Stein publicly reaffirms her attachment to the America she chose to leave decades ago: "There is something in this native land business and you cannot get away from it, in peace time you do not seem to notice it much particularly when you live in foreign parts but when there is a war and you are all alone and completely cut off from knowing about your country well then there it is, your native land is your native land, it certainly is" (*WIHS* 250). Here, it seems that World War II has intensified and clarified her attachment to her native land. The literal and figurative return to America chronicled in *Everybody's Autobiography* is developed and brought to a satisfying conclusion.

Stein's expatriatism is not merely a rejection of America; it is a strategy that allows her to be more absorbed in her Americanism — a way, paradoxically, to define her patriotism *through* her expatriatism. Catherine Parke points to the duality that defines Stein as both part of and apart from place: "part patriot" and "part expatriate" (556). Her rejection of repatriation, even during her intensified nationalism at the ending of World War II underscores her insistence on this double status: "It is a charming thought, ten days after the landing in France the American authorities seem to be quite certain that as soon as they like they can repatriate all Americans still in France. We giggled we said that is optimism" (*WIHS* 200). She glories in "hav[ing] two countries to be proud of that belong to [me]"—America and France (*WIHS* 243).

Stein exemplifies "the exile's oddly indeterminate status: of being imaginatively neither *here* nor *there*" (Kennedy, "Place" 514), physically in Paris, but "internally" in America. Translating geography into a personal issue, her Americanism, she transcends the limits of geographical place. *Everybody's Autobiography* repeats on a grand scale Stein's tendency to merge the highly personal and eccentric with the general and collective. This process systematically legitimizes her universalized point of view on

Americans. Her logic masquerades as authoritative statements that are at once individualistic and collective, personal and generic, unique and representative.

Stein explains her dual nationality in *Paris France* (1940), the memoir and tribute to her adopted country written several years after *Everybody's Autobiography*. Geography of place reflects geography of the mind, the separated countries mirroring the split between her private and public worlds. One country, she says, is to write about and one is to live in: "After all everybody, that is, everybody who writes is interested in living inside themselves in order to tell what is inside themselves. That is why writers have to have two countries, the one where they belong and the one in which they live really. The second one is romantic, it is separate from themselves, it is not real but it is really there" (*PF* 2). Significantly, Stein avoids using "I," choosing instead to cloak her original theory about the motives behind expatriation under what "everybody" or unspecified "writers" need. Her explanation for why expatriation is mandatory for "everybody who writes" hinges entirely upon one subtle assumption: that people who wish to "tell what is inside themselves ... have to have two countries." She explained to the French newspaper the *Intransigeant* that she liked to live in France because "your life can belong to you" (*EA* 102–03): there, she *could* live inside herself, whereas living in America constantly forced her recognition and remembrance of past selves and the emotional trauma that she inevitably associates with those selves. In *Paris France* she notes that "publicity in France is really not important, tradition and their private life and the soil which always produces something, that is what counts" (10). She more thoroughly than in *Everybody's Autobiography* explains the particular advantage of being a writer in France. The French "respect art and letters," endow writers and other artists with "privileges" (*PF* 21), and "surround you with a civilised atmosphere and [the French] leave you inside of you completely to yourself" (57). Stein has so much confidence in her status as a writer living in France that she is able, during the German occupation, to declare to a stranger in a train station, "I am a writer and so the French people take care of me" (*WIHS* 119).

For Stein, France provides refuge for the writing self and America provides material for writing, but she never acknowledges this odd version of expatriation as her own invention, passing it off instead as a general truth for "everybody" or "everybody who writes." Because writing about America even from great distances in time and space evokes memories of selves that exist in relation to other people (for example, childhood or her student days at Radcliffe), she enacts on a physical level that

separation of selves by living apart from the country most dear and emotionally threatening to her.

Speaking as a representative member of her American generation, she
rationalizes her choice to expatriate as a collective rather than an idiosyncratic act: "The English Victorians were like that about Italy, the early
nineteenth century Americans were like that about Spain, the middle nineteenth century Americans were like that about England, my generation the
end of the nineteenth century American generation was like that about
France" (*PF* 2). Her identification with the tendencies of the American
expatriate generation born around the turn of the century converts her
choice into a natural, repetitive human action visible across generations
and cultures. The established pattern, "like that about," takes on the force
of a natural, inevitable human tendency to which she, like all human
beings, is subject. But this peculiar theory about why a writer must have
two countries is, nevertheless, Stein's own. She gives the illusion of uphold-
ing a tradition while setting a precedent. Thus, her views appear as both
"natural" and uniquely American.

Exile allowed her to be "more intensely alone with [her] eyes and
[her] English" (*ABT* 70), to focus on her own perceptions rather than on
translating the perceptions of others. For Stein, "french [*sic*] is a spoken
language and English a written one.... French is a spoken language English really is not" (*PF* 5). In France, "they read more with their ears than
with their eyes," but in English "we read more with our eyes than with our
ears" (*EA* 17). Extending this generalization further, she interprets the
American experience as primarily visual, attributing to the emphasis on
sight otherwise inexplicable practices: Americans, she claims, want to make
everything something anybody can see by looking.

> That is very interesting, that is the reason there are no fences in
> between no walls to hide anything no curtains to cover anything and
> the cinema that can make anything be anything anybody can see by
> looking [perhaps a reference to the vulnerability Stein felt when seeing
> herself in a newsreel]. That is the way it is [196].

Stein interprets in spatial terms the openness or unself-conscious-
ness of Americans, their failure to place visible boundaries on the landscape or conceal their private space. Thomas Couser argues that she associates "the lack of privacy" with "the democratic way of life" (*American
Autobiography* 155). Her pronouncement that "windows in a building are
the most interesting thing in America" (183) suggests her fascination with
what she interprets as the American desire not to "hide" or "cover" anything, as symbolized by transparent boundaries. Once she identifies an

attribute as typically American, she filters generalizations and common-place observations through that attribute. This eccentric logic constructs incrementally Stein's personalized, generic portrait of the typical American. She ignores the restrictions of causal logic and identifies something as American simply because she observes it in America; she then subsequently derives other American tendencies from that original premise.[23] As in her system of attributing essential traits to people based on state of origin, for example, she creates an apparently logical, but faulty, formula. Again, she does this by appropriating the right to define the terms, in this case the term American. Stating that Americans are "slow minded" (277) or that Virginia and California "make anybody know what was American" (249), for example, professes only a superficial logic obviously based on subjective observation.

Defining herself as the representative American necessarily requires defining the American people as a group. The chapter "America" catalogues Stein's American experience, which includes an examination of the eating, standing, and speaking patterns of Americans.[24] Dismissing social, genetic, and historical influence, she attributes the makeup of a person to the physical environment: "After all anybody is as their land and air is" (*HWW* 80 and *WIHS* 258). Her adamant belief in a system of categorizing Americans according to their physical environment maintains that differences in physical features, such as the roundness of the head or the position of the eyes in relation to the nose, "has to do with what the land looks like and what it can grow" (*HWW* 81). In *Paris France*, notes J. Gerald Kennedy, Stein employs similar tactics, portraying Paris by "isolat[ing] essential qualities reflected by gestures, habits, or attitudes" (Kennedy, *Imagining* 44). Such generalizations about the American character and appearance undermine any pretense Stein may have to an authoritative view.

Stein's definitions for *America* and *Americanism*, then, are not logically convincing, but her reliance on terms and phrases defined earlier in the text that characterize American-ness (e.g., slow-minded, wait, quickly clear) lends a deceptive veneer to her logic: "[B]ut anyway I am clear I am a good American, I am slow-minded and quickly clear in expression, I am certain that I see everything that is seen and in between I stand around but I do not wait, no American can wait he can stand around and do nothing but he can not wait, that is why he is not like Milton who served by standing and waiting" (*EA* 301). Here, Stein clearly distinguishes between American and English traditions and tendencies. The reference to Milton establishes a double parallel — English to American literary tradition and English literary genius to herself as a twentieth-century American literary genius. Like Milton, she waited for recognition while in inner-exile from her country. She conflates the definitions of an American and of herself (both of whom "can not wait") and dismantles the logical definition process: Is she or is "the American" the model or prior category? The inverted logic dismantles and confuses the links between cause and effect, between the influencer and influenced, and between the originator and originated. Does Stein's exemplification of American characteristics — her self-ascribed slow-mindedness and impatience — make her distinctly American? Or does the typical American duplicate *her* attributes? In Steinian logic, anything American is self-derived from and equated with Stein. Stein equals America; therefore, by extension *Steinian* means "American."

Stein's self-legitimized and self-proclaimed genius complements her Americanism. Her insecurity over her status as genius duplicates her anxiety over nearly not being born: "And if you stop writing if you are a genius and you have stopped writing are you still one if you have stopped writing. I do wonder about that thing" (*EA* 85). Even free from the tyranny of public identity and safe within the private world of writing and being a genius, she "wondered" about the instability of selfhood. Could something as unpredictable and uncontrollable as her temporary inability to write (as happened after the publication of *The Autobiography*) threaten her carefully constructed sense of inner self? Defining genius with a series of unquestioned premises that encompass her personal artistic goals, she renounces the historian's and autobiographer's role and exempts herself forever from the obligations of remembering and recording, obligations that Hellman accepts and Shepard depends on emotionally: a genius "does not have to remember the two hundred years that everybody else has to remember" (121). Although the demands of the genre require remembering and identity, she rejects and theoretically escapes both activities: a genius lives in "a reality that has nothing to do with the passage of time" (154), and needs no "internal recognition of time" (*EA* 243). Stein's definition of "genius," like that of "American," reinforces rather than explains her tendencies and preferences.

Genius and *Americanism* defined as interdependent Steinian terms enable her to formulate the Stein-America equation. Her convoluted, self-serving logic attributes importance to generations, places, and influences simply because they mirror her own attributes or conditions; the logic traces the reciprocal definition process taking place between America and herself. She identifies herself with America, the still-young nation, with a Whitmanesque stroke: "[G]enius has to be made in a country which is forming itself to be what it is but is not yet ... not yet common property"

(92). This implacable Steinian logic leads to the conclusion that just as "Einstein was the creative philosophic mind of the century," she is "the creative literary mind of the century" (21–22).

Stein's Reconciliation of Identity and Entity

By the close of *Everybody's Autobiography*, Stein's ideas on the nature of the self have evolved and signal a less anxious attitude toward the identity-entity split. Even after returning from America, however, she was still haunted by the question of identity: "Settled down in Bilignin I became worried about identity and remembered Mother Goose, I am I because my little dog knows me and I was not sure but that that only proved the dog was he and not that I was I" (297). Only the subject that confers identity has the power to affirm existence. The "I" upon whom identity is conferred (e.g., a celebrity) is powerless and doomed to doubt existence. But through her American tour, Stein resolves her concern about the personal versus the public right to define "I." She concedes that "perhaps after all they are right the Americans in being more interested in you than in the work you have done" (90). The closing lines of *Everybody's Autobiography* very nearly dismisses the recurring dilemma of identity: "[P]erhaps I am not I even if my little dog knows me." That Stein closes her text firmly in the continuous present formally marks the reconciliation of past and present, the self of memory and the self of the moment: "I like what I have and now it is today."

Ultimately reversing the disassociation of self and place most dramatically symbolized by her expatriation, she defines the self through America and takes into account its tangible geographical features as well as its abstract meaning. The oscillation of *Everybody's Autobiography* between self-portraiture and portraiture of the American people produces Stein as both an individualistic, self-engendered American genius and as the collective American "everybody" of the title.

CHAPTER THREE

Lillian Hellman's
Scoundrel Time *and*
the Ownership of Memory

Who owns memory? Lillian Hellman's *Scoundrel Time* (1976) focuses on this central quandary of the autobiographical genre and poses questions about reading practices, authority, and accountability. Are autobiographers whose texts necessarily deal in historical fact more bound to the public's genre expectations than chroniclers who limit autobiography to personal, unverifiable or insignificant history? Is Hellman's accountability intensified because *Scoundrel Time* deals with historical fact rather than introspective, private concerns? Does Hellman's confrontational, public style, which challenges the premise of truth-value in a text, leave her more open to criticism than more conventional autobiographers? In equating herself with America, the ideal, does Hellman, like Stein, endow herself with special privileges or responsibilities as an autobiographer? Where do we draw the line as to how far an author can go in claiming America as her own invention — to hold up and insist on her version as the authoritative one?

Critical debate since the publication of *Scoundrel Time* documents the effect of Hellman's unorthodox autobiographical method, which melds historical events with material and techniques often dismissed as "feminine" — that is, impressionistic, personal reflections and therefore not genuine autobiography. The acrimonious disputes still raging over her interpretation of the McCarthy era testify to the volatility of her text.[1] But in a large sense, the bitter fight demonstrates the confusion and anger that the contemporary autobiographical act can provoke when an author so publicly and adamantly claims ownership of her own memory in a text the public labels contemporary history. Near the end of her life, her insistence on writing her version of America — on reinventing it in ideal terms — is her way of fixing and preserving an ideal America which is as much a myth as Stein's or Shepard's.

In this third volume of her memoirs Hellman takes on the role of official "rememberer" and becomes the repository and validator of American values. *Scoundrel Time*, like her other memoirs, *An Unfinished Woman* (1969), *Pentimento* (1973), and *Maybe* (1980), examines the nature of memory as much as it reconstructs it. She rejects and condemns contemporary America's failure or refusal to remember its own history and appoints herself as the one American who *will* keep much of the past in her head. This position is diametrically opposed to Stein's rejection of the role of rememberer, recorder, or historian — the caretaker of memory. Stein's attempt to live solely in the realm of genius, immune to time, constitutes a rejection of history, an escape from the narrative act that Hellman masters and exploits. Unlike Stein, who in her life simultaneously feared and desired celebrity and struggled to keep the "inside" and "outside" of identity separate, Hellman gloried in the power of being a celebrity.

Hellman also exploits the reader's predetermined responses to traditional American values as she appropriates America itself as her ideology. Like Stein in *Everybody's Autobiography*, Hellman resurrects an idealized, privately conceived America; however, hers is not the quirky, self-invented America of an eccentric exile, but an affirmation of the familiar America of school children's history books — a synthetic memory woven from the "American Dream" sought by generations. Hellman alludes in the opening of *Scoundrel Time* to her deliberate timing in writing her memoir and notes her two previous unsuccessful attempts "to write about what has come to be known as the McCarthy period" (603).[2] Her diminished reluctance to write also surfaces in an interview just a year before the publication of *Scoundrel Time* and perhaps signals a turning point; she denounces the "relativistic morality" prevalent in America (de Pue in Bryer 190). Clearly, she wants to recover the simplistic, authentic, yet anachronistic America that corresponds with her upbringing, moral code, and early radical politics. Hellman's concept of America is founded on known, dependable, and culturally endorsed values. She espouses the traditional values of an ideal America as the origins and shapers of her character and as the logic behind her decision not to name names to the House Un-American Activities Committee.[3]

More than an historical record, *Scoundrel Time* is Hellman's manifesto about controlling access to her own memory and its relation to historical fact. The assertions in her famous May 19, 1952, letter to HUAC chair John S. Wood,[4] the debate evoked by the publication of *Scoundrel Time*, and the control of memory in autobiography present analogous issues. All three represent the autobiographer's assertion of *her* memories as an authoritative version of the truth on the historical, personal, and generic levels. Thus, in an act no less heroic than her stand before HUAC, in *Scoundrel Time*, Hellman claims the right to a series of crucial activities, including writing her own truth without deference to the demands of history and corrupt politics, publicly acknowledging counterculture political views, and responding to harsh critics without offering the apology demanded of her for 25 years.

A passage from the letter to Wood, dated just two days before her HUAC appearance and printed in its entirety in *Scoundrel Time*, encapsulates Hellman's messianic Americanism, cunning rhetoric, identification with America, and genuine idealism. The passage reveals, in essence, the enigmatic subtext at work in *Scoundrel Time* and in every aspect of her complex private and public life.

> I was raised in an old-fashioned American tradition and there were certain homely things that were taught to me: to try to tell the truth, not to bear false witness, not to harm my neighbor, to be loyal to my country, and so on. In general, I respected these ideals of Christian honor and did as well with them as I knew how. It is my belief that you will agree with these simple rules of human decency and will not expect me to violate the good American tradition from which they spring. I would, therefore, like to come before you and speak of myself [659–60].

She refuses to reconstruct, edit, or rearrange her memory into the self-incriminating personal historical narrative HUAC seeks. Her courageous but not unprecedented[5] refusal to name names — to waive her right to plead the Fifth Amendment and not to "bring bad trouble to people," as her letter states — constitutes her assertive claim to her own memory even more than it constitutes the conventional political or moral statements debated, praised, or repudiated by her peers since 1976.[6] Ingeniously, Hellman appears the compliant witness, agrees to go before the committee and speak only of herself, and offers her memory on her own terms, all the while turning the committee's challenge of *her* Americanism into her challenge of *their* Americanism.

Ironically, the letter became public property during the hearing, much to the distress of the committee. After Hellman requested permission to refer to the letter and expressed hope that the committee would "reconsider" (672) the offer made in the letter, Mr. Wood ordered the letter into the hearing records: "Mr. Tavenner did just that, and when he had finished Rauh sprang to his feet, picked up a stack of mimeographed copies of my letter, and handed them out to the press section. I was puzzled by this — I hadn't noticed he had the copies — but I did notice that Rauh was looking happy. ... Mr. Tavenner was upset" (673).

Thus, the sudden entry of her letter into the public domain broadcast the committee's demand that she cooperate with their appropriation of her memory and announced, inadvertently, that their demand, made in the name of Americanism, in itself violates "the good American tradition." She cleverly exposes the paradoxical position HUAC forces her into: she must relinquish "the good American tradition," not to harm others, to prove her Americanism. Reliance on the glittering generalities that constitute the American public's America gains her tacit permission to define the terms under which her memory will be made public property. She assumes in writing that the committee agrees with the "simple rules of human decency" and would never, therefore, encourage her "to violate the good American tradition from which they spring."

The meekness and reasonableness of her phrasing in the letter, "I would, therefore, like to come before you and speak of myself," renders the committee's refusal of her request a tacit self-indictment of their own un–Americanism. Her phrasing, an allusion to the oath given in courts of law — "to tell the truth, the whole truth, and nothing but the truth" — simultaneously aligns her with American, moral, Christian, and legal principles while it defends her against the accusation of un–American activities. The moral impact of her intention "to try to tell the truth" intensifies when one considers her vulnerable position at the time she wrote the letter and the accusations of falsification, lying, misleading, fictionalizing, and self-aggrandizement that followed the publication of *Scoundrel Time*.

Hellman's conflation of "old-fashioned American tradition," "ideals of Christian honor," "loyalty" to America, and "simple rules of human decency" also forecasts her conversion in the post–McCarthy years from liberalism to a new generic ethos free of political or religious connotations. In a "country that cries out for belief and ... has none" (679), Hellman reconstructs her Americanism and replaces her liberalism, Jewishness, or Puritanism with "something private called, for want of something that should be more accurate, decency" (679). As her friend John Hersey puts it, her code narrows down to an insistence of "decency in human transactions" (26).

The associations in *Scoundrel Time* between autobiography and dissent, and between American ideology and dissent culminate for her in a characteristic act of rebellion that in the end dominates her memoir's historical impact. She herself admits that the text is not the typical "history"— "a mishmash of early influences, books read, what teacher taught you what and when, even what you looked like" (613)—but *her* "history of the time" (607). Paradoxically, even as she intends to "stick to what I know" (607) and subsequently revises the American collective memory, she chronicles her loss of faith in "truth," "facts," and the genre whose very title means "memory."

The Geographics of Memory: An Ideal America

Even more than the committee hearing and other assorted musings on the 1950s in America, the "hours of the deer" is the silent emotional center of *Scoundrel Time*, a private geography where all the strands of Hellman's life retrospectively intertwine. It is the locus of loss — of land and an ideal American way of life, of Hammett, and of her past selves. Just as her appearance before HUAC functions as the public and political high point of *Scoundrel Time*, the "hours of the deer" represents the book's emotional crescendo. This moving scene recounts the visit of large herds of wild deer to the farmhouse at Hellman and Hammett's beloved Hardscrabble Farm in Pleasantville, New York. It is an unlikely piece to include in what purports to be a political memoir, but suggests how completely emotion and stark fact often merge for her.

The physicality of America is an abstraction for Stein in her expatriation until made real by her American tour, and is both palpable and symbolic for Shepard. However, for Hellman, significant locations represent ways of life, phases of work or relationships more than actual places. Hellman's sense of physical place in America is only occasionally significant in her memoirs (e.g., the fig tree in *Pentimento*, associated with her coming of age). She converts place into abstractions, aspects of herself that transcend geography, and subordinates the physicality of place to what she experiences in that place. *Scoundrel Time* focuses primarily on one significant place, Hardscrabble Farm, where her professional and personal life flowered. Her relationship to the farm is one of existential insideness, a condition that geographer Edward Relph calls "the deep and complete identity with a place that is the very foundation of the place concept" (55). In microcosm, the farm is the realization of the ideology that constitutes Hellman's America. By recounting in intricate factual and emotional detail the sale of the farm to pay attorneys' fees before her HUAC appearance and blacklisting in Hollywood, she recapitulates the fall of America as epitomized by the McCarthy era and Watergate. She also savors, sacralizes, and renders untouchable what is good about that time and place. The farm is the intersection of emotional and political geography, a place where she maps emotional loss, although part of the memory may be fiction.

Hellman's memory links the loss of the farm, the end of a successful professional era (she purchased Hardscrabble Farm with money earned from *The Little Foxes*), and the evils of the McCarthy period. *Scoundrel Time* documents in detail the reasons she and Dashiell Hammett were forced to sell the farm, as well as the actual sale and dispersal of all its equipment. She also documents her emotions throughout that period, noting the loss of the farm as "the most painful loss of my life" (680). The loss was so traumatic that she repressed the memories connected with it for years. In the chapter in *An Unfinished Woman* about her visit to Russia in the mid–1960s, Hellman describes the flood of touching memories about the farm that surface during a night she drinks vodka alone in her hotel room. She lets the memories come: "They were not bad memories, most of them ... but I knew that I had taken a whole period of my life and thrown it somewhere, always intending to call for it again, but now that it came time to call, I couldn't remember where I had left it" (184).

The loss of the farm, a metaphor for rural America in perfect combination with the intellectual life, meant many things to Hellman. But primarily, the loss signaled the end of a way of life. Hellman had thrived there: she had written four plays and four or five movies (*UW* 185). She and Hammett spent the best of their years together there (*UW* 133); and she operated at optimum energy, becoming the "woman who worked from seven in the morning until two or three the next morning and woke rested and hungry for each new day" (*UW* 185). The loss of Hardscrabble Farm is also a loss of her former productive self: she knew she "could never again be that woman" (*UW* 185). Hellman and Hammett's refusal to subdivide the property to sell it points to the moral principles that define their connection to the land and their idealistic need to protect the land and the way of life it represents. Hellman attributes their decision to Hammett's insistence that they not join in the pervasive degradation of the land: "Let everybody else spoil the land. Let's you and I leave it alone. Let somebody else do it. I don't want to spoil this land" (Berger in Bryer 260).[7]

The visit of the large groups of wild deer to the farm house a mere "five days before the storage people were to come for the furniture" is "so stunning, so unbelievable" (682), so much like a fantasy, that one questions the extent to which Hellman's memory rearranged the events. The strong adjectives signal that her description probably serves emotional truth rather than strict fact.

> On the wide road from the lake at least twenty deer, moving slowly, were joining a larger group who were wandering up the shorter path through the fruit trees. All of them, small and large, pale and darker, moved without fear, stopping along the way to nibble at the May buds. Eight of them had moved close to the terrace, were looking up at the house, but without curiosity, as if it were another kind of tree. Then a group of them went past the terrace [683].

In this profoundly serene scene converge many disparate elements for Hellman in a difficult time in her life; it is a period of communion between her and Hammett and the soon-to-be abandoned land, between Hammett and herself, and between Hellman and Hammett and the fearless deer who represent nature's approach to the human world. Foreshadowing the house's "disappearance" from Hellman's life, the natural setting figuratively reabsorbs the house by transforming it into "another kind of tree." The unverifiability of the scene renders it a more poignant goodbye; only Hammett, long dead at the writing of *Scoundrel Time*, shared that memory with her. Therefore, what Hellman deemed the "finest sight" of her life remains hers alone to remember, repress, or rewrite (682).

In terms of historical narrative and financial repercussions, the sale of the farm is the end of an era for her and Hammett, but it is also the emotional intersection for all the strands of memory that Hellman explores in writing memoirs. The deer scene functions, in mythical terms, as a sacred space, the meeting place of the human and the divine spheres. It is a private moment in which she and Hammett escape the clutches of history and scoundrel time. Pristine and unverifiable, the scene distills the best of their relationship. It is at once a heartbreaking loss and a joyous recovery: the prelude to Hellman's hard financial times and Hammett's last sick years, but also an eternally recoverable personal truth. The "hours of the deer" (683) are a mental place to which she can return, her equivalent to the transcendent "stillness" Shepard experiences when alone with the landscape.

The pattern of silent understanding prevalent in Hellman and Hammett's long relationship dominates the reverent hours of that late afternoon and continues into the night. Hellman stifles her emotional nature in deference to Hammett's reticence. Their interaction subdues and "tames" Hellman. The scene begins with Hammett's verbal command for quiet:

> Hammett came to the foot of the stairs and in a whisper said, "Come
> down. Be very quiet. When you get to the last few steps, crouch very
> low so that you can't be seen through the window" [682].

Soon he resorts to actual physical restraint of her emotions: Hammett
"put his hand over [her] mouth" to stop the "choking sounds" she begins
to make (682). Once Hellman complies with the physical restraint by
silencing herself, Hammett's actions diminish to paternal pats on the
head.

During those two or three "hours of the deer," Hellman and Hammett experience an intense communion, but the intimacy seems to depend
on her childlike compliance with the role Hammett writes for her: "Neither Hammett nor I had said a word during the hours of the deer, but I
guess I made sounds once in a while, because he would laugh and pat my
head" (683). After a dinner later that evening during which they did not
speak, Hellman ventures an oblique reference to the intensely emotional
event they had shared: "We had something nice. Who managed that?"
(684). However, Hammett merely smiles and turns his face from Hellman
in answer, a paradigmatic moment in an intimacy that was a delicate balance of silence and speech, absence and presence.

Interestingly, in *Scoundrel Time*, Hellman alters the date of the sale
of the farm from 1951 to 1952. What could be the motive for this alteration? Was it conscious? Placing the loss of the farm after her committee
appearance directly attributes the sale to the evils of HUAC and the IRS,
which demanded back taxes, and emphasizes the persecution she felt. Even
more significantly, the change conveniently dovetails into a narrative portraying her and Hammett as innocents cast out from Eden and Joseph
McCarthy and his men as the villains. In other words, the alteration conveys a deeper, personal truth: the emotional devastation the era had on
Hellman. Carl Rollyson cynically asserts that the mistaken date is a deliberate error made only for self-promoting reasons: "Always one to make a
story better, in *Scoundrel Time* she puts her selling of Hardscrabble Farm
in 1952, after her testimony before HUAC. Actually, the farm was gone by
the end of 1951. She knew her idyll in Pleasantville was over" (317). She
states in *Scoundrel Time* that she first put the farm up for sale when "Rauh
asked for and got a delay in my appearance before the Committee"
(627–28), thus clearly placing the farm still in her possession in spring
1952, after her subpoena. But in a 1979 interview, she states unequivocally,
"I sold it one month before I testified [i.e., April 1952]" (Berger in Bryer
259). Also in the Berger interview, she retells the "hours of the deer" and
places the event on "an April afternoon," meaning the April previous to

May 1952, the month of her appearance, "three days before we moved" (despite the fact that the deer nibble "May buds").

Much more interesting than whether or not she consciously invented the scene is her possible need to do so, an intriguing motive ignored by biographers and literary critics alike.[8] If she and Hammett had already vacated the farmhouse months before in 1951 (as Rollyson and others point out), she either substantially altered the events or fabricated the "hours of the deer" entirely. She calls the visitation of the deer "a great farewell gift." Was this gift one to herself? Was her idyllic vision her way of erasing the pain associated with the farm, Hammett, and the downturn in her professional life? This "remarkable" visitation of the deer transforms her pain into hope and signifies the merely temporary effect that HUAC had on her happiness: "[The hours of the deer] turned pain into something else, something almost good, a gift that made me think maybe luck was not gone forever and past punishment might someday be of little importance" (*ST* 680–81). She explains that in all the years she and Hammett lived there, although there were numerous deer on the property, they had seen only one deer, about ten years before, near the house: "They were always in the woods, way in the woods. And you had to hunt for a long, long time before you found them" (Berger in Bryer 258). The improbability of such a visit casts an almost supernatural mood over her account.

Like a microcosmic Eden, a memory of a lost paradise no one else can ever verify or disprove, the house, gardens, and woods at Hardscrabble Farm encapsulate the ideal relationship, workplace, haven, and living space — a way of life Hellman and Hammett were forced to relinquish. However, Hellman's characteristic optimism eventually transforms the sale of the farm and house into something more than mere "loss." The farm's private geography allows Hellman a belated personal and political triumph. She philosophizes that "a time of [her] life had ended" and focuses on adjusting to her "altered way of living" (680). The "hours of the deer" may be her therapeutic way of rewriting the past into what she *wants* to remember. Chronicling in detail the last day she lived on the farm, a Monday when people collected the numerous farm implements and items she was forced to sell, she remembers the pain, but overcomes it with an appreciative refusal to dwell on loss and the past, and with an insistence on merging the "then" and "now": "I knew that day I would never have any of them again. But whenever I said that to myself I also said that I was lucky ever to have had them at all, and that is what I feel today, these many years later" (692). She affirms, late in life, through the invention of a private, ideal geography, what cannot be lost or threatened by HUAC—

honor, love, the value of work, the joy of working the land, and a unique professional collaboration.

"The hours of the deer," whether real or imagined, epitomizes Hellman's immersion in and fascination with the processes of memory. This fascination with memory opposes Stein's aversion to the endless forgetting and remembering associated with history and identity. As in Stein's *Everybody's Autobiography*, the writing act in Hellman's text transcends the subject matter. The continual exploration and redefinition of memory in *Scoundrel Time* supersede the traditional intentions of autobiography. Referring in a 1980 interview to *Maybe*, her fourth memoir, she indicates her long-term preoccupation with memory in her work: "I want always to go back to the theme of this book. To memory. To What is memory? Where does memory fit? Who and what influences or changes memory?" (Warga in Bryer 279). She organizes *Scoundrel Time* according to the subjective workings of memory rather than around a chronology of the McCarthy period, an approach that in itself is unorthodox for a political memoir. She sanctions this erratic method in the text itself: "It is impossible to write about any part of the McCarthy period in a clear-dated, annotated form; much crossed with much else, nothing obeyed a neat plan" (642). This achronological approach reflects her belief that "nothing begins when you think it did" (*UW* 132), and it betrays her feeling that the chronological narrative of traditional autobiography is inadequate for her purposes.

Much of the controversy over the political memoir arises from the vast discrepancy between Hellman's and her public's understanding of the function of autobiographical writings. She had definite views about the very word "autobiography," and the simultaneous bitter denunciation and high praise accorded her memoirs demonstrate that she pushes both historical and poetic narrative to their limits. Her reasons for preferring the word *memoir* over *autobiography* for *An Unfinished Woman* might easily also apply to *Scoundrel Time*. She insists that the text is "not an autobiography at all" and that she chose the word *memoir*, it seems, by default: "I have chosen the word *memoir* which is an old word and a not very good word because I couldn't find any other word that seemed right.... It starts at the beginning so called and does all kinds of jumps.... It has no chronology.... [I]t isn't about me in the usual sense, in the autobiographical sense" (Gardner in Bryer 123). She contends that *Pentimento*, too, is not an autobiography but a memoir, something "quite different" (Albert in Bryer 176). She has "no interest in writing" (176) autobiography proper and her inability to "find any other word that seemed right" highlights her casual attitude toward the invention of a genre to suit her purposes. Essential to her definition of autobiography are a focus on the self and "space control —

when this happened and how it happened and what followed next." Because
Pentimento "doesn't follow any plan or place" (176), she differentiates it
from "autobiography." Obviously, her distinction between autobiography
and memoir hinges on whether or not the work follows sequential chronology. Thus, all her memoirs, memories presented in an associative or
impressionistic order that mirrors subjective human experience, fit her
all-purpose category *memoir* more precisely than they fit her version of the
term *autobiography*.

The title of her fourth memoir, *Maybe, A Story* (a hybrid of autobiography and novel), indicates the tentativeness with which Hellman
approaches the genre and her acute awareness of the public's expectations
for what Elizabeth Bruss calls "truth-value" in autobiography ("Eye" 299),
in particular, its consistency with outside evidence. The subtitle, *A Story*,
immediately warns the reader of the book's ambiguous genre status and
protects her in advance from vicious charges of fabrication. By the time
she published it, a mere one year after the emended version of *Scoundrel
Time* appeared in *Three*, she had witnessed the attacks on all three of her
previous memoirs. So, in a defensive, strategic gesture in *Maybe*, she
addresses prior and anticipated criticism — charges of vagueness, inaccuracy, and lies — and clarifies her definition of memoir *within* the memoir
itself. In one of the many italicized sections of the text, Hellman digresses
from the central plotline and contemplates the interdependent processes
of writing and memory:

> It goes without saying that in their memoirs people should try to tell
> the truth as they see it or else what's the sense? Maybe time blurs or
> changes things for them. But you try, anyway. In the three memoir
> books I wrote, I tried very hard for the truth. I did try, but here I don't
> know much of what really happened and never tried to find out. In
> addition to the ordinary deceptions that you and others make in your
> life, time itself makes time fuzzy and meshes truth with half truth
> [*M* 50–51; passage in italics].

Hellman first presents a seemingly traditional dictum: memoirists "should
try to tell the truth as they see it." She establishes "what is remembered"
as an absolute irrespective of its relation to fact. As Paul John Eakin
explains, the issue of truth in autobiography is not "a simple opposition
between fiction and fact, since fiction can have for the author ... the status of remembered fact (remembering something that is not true ...)"
(*Fictions* 17). In fact, in an interview with Christine Doudna the year
Scoundrel Time appeared, Hellman distinguishes memory from fact:
"Memory, of course, is not the same thing as what really happened in the

minute of pleasure or pain. Pain can almost totally fade. And another much lesser pain is much more easily remembered and more important to you. What is intensely important can, when the years have passed, fade, disappear" (Bryer 200). *Maybe* announces her satisfaction with an "inconclusive rhetorical stance" (Adams, *Telling* 129). It can be read as her final, personal "resolute, self-satisfying, self-defining *maybe*" (Adams 129) *and* as an unmistakable assertion that she need not justify herself on the subject of truth. But in the largest sense, it is Hellman's personal and public showdown with the anathema of memory.

The title of *Scoundrel Time* takes on yet another meaning when she blames "time itself" for making chronology "fuzzy" and "mesh[ing] truth with half truth." Time itself erodes memory; rather than bringing precision and wisdom it brings only a growing knowledge of one's ignorance of life: "as one grows older, one realizes how little one knows about any relationship, or even about oneself" (*M* 11). She points out the two inevitable sources of inaccuracy in remembering and uses the innocuous second-person to excuse the "ordinary deceptions that you and others make in your life." If one cannot trust one's own memory, she asks, then upon whose memory are we to construct truth? And who decides? The erosion of memory presents a tangle of contradictions: even if dedicated to writing truth, the memoirist is increasingly aware of the impossibility of doing so, ever more aware that Hellman's "childish belief in absolutes" is indeed childish (*M* 51).

During a span of more than forty years, Hellman's philosophy on writing evolved from an absolutist, messianic vision to the existential one in *Maybe*. *Scoundrel Time* represents the major transition point in that dramatic evolution forced on her to some degree by the derisive reactions of her readers. By the time she confronted the McCarthy era on paper, she could skeptically demote truth: "Truth made you a traitor as it often does in a time of scoundrels" (651). However, a transition from an absolutist belief in truth early in her career to an abandonment of the pursuit of truth in *Maybe* emphasizes that profound change even more. In a 1939 interview, she states that "if a person doesn't want to involve himself with the truth he has no business trying to write at all" (Beebe in Bryer 9). At the beginning of her career as a playwright, she reveals her allegiance to truth in the ideological, absolute sense; we can arrive at, examine, pursue, and communicate truth. It is a public, collective commodity rather than a private, subjective pursuit. In her early philosophy, truth with its almost holy connotations must reside at the center of a writer's work: "Some sort of truth, profound or trivial, but the truth must be the main objective of any one who seeks a form of literary expression" (Beebe in

Bryer 9). For her, "good writing" includes a political aspect; it must be "propaganda" in the uncorrupted sense of the word (Beebe in Bryer 9).

By 1968 she openly acknowledges the slipperiness of truth, but still views it as an absolute: "How do you know if you're telling the truth" about the dead people about whom you write? And she admits, "I always wonder if I'm telling the truth" (Chusmir in Bryer 163, 164). By the time she wrote *Maybe*, she had effectively abandoned memory as a source of certainty: "[A]s time and much of life has passed, my memory — which for the purpose of this tale has kept me awake sorting out what I am certain of, what maybe I added to what, because I didn't see or know the people — won't supply what I need to know" (*M* 63). It may be that Hellman's refusal to consider the enigmatic nature of memory as something she was personally and morally responsible for only further incited attacks on her character.

Hellman's repeated statements that she wrote her own, not her nation's, history sufficiently explain (for the legions who need explanation) her unique autobiographical project. It is only fair to say that readers themselves carry a portion of responsibility for the purported "sins" against the truth in the pages of *Scoundrel Time*. The problem arises in part because critics have too often removed *Scoundrel Time* from the context of her other memoirs as if it were a total departure from them. On the contrary, the text extends the intentions, metaphors, and exploration of memory found in *An Unfinished Woman* and *Pentimento*, and it is also the precursor of the abandonment of truth in *Maybe*, whose indeterminate genre status is Hellman's ingenious final rebuff to the demand for historical truth. When resituated in the context of her complete four-volume, 17-year autobiographical project, the cumulative power of *Scoundrel Time* effectively counteracts even the most malicious criticism.[9]

Timothy Dow Adams identifies the central problem of truth-value in *Scoundrel Time* when he observes that the text "has been judged as if it were legal testimony" (*Telling* 159). Bernard Dick defends the memoir by pointing out the obvious, that the text is "an impressionistic view of history" (157), beyond a narrow reading of the text as journalism or history. Anita Grossman mentions the difficulty of reconciling Hellman's "moral vision" with the expectations of the genre (305). Her remark tacitly validates the public's unfair expectations of historical truth over Hellman's acknowledged intentions. In the 1979 italicized emendations that close *Scoundrel Time*, Hellman, perhaps exasperated with the whole issue of her questionable moral heroism, manages an unexpected retort to the numerous critics who accuse her of portraying herself as a moral heroine.[10] She insists that in the book she "tried to avoid ... what is called a moral stand"

(726). However, her emendation dramatically reverses that decision: "I'd like to take that stand now" (726).

After several failed attempts to recount the events of the McCarthy era, she gives priority to the subjective, a choice that provoked disproportionate fury. Hilton Kramer may be correct in saying that she made "theater" of her life and treated herself as a "fictional character" (5).[11] But he and other Hellman adversaries have derived years of theatrical self-aggrandizement in print by reiterating and embellishing that very accusation. One can even agree that at times she fails to distinguish "distortion from reflection" (Billson and Smith 179), but these sins, it may be argued, are common to all memoirists. Even before the publication of *Scoundrel Time*, she makes clear that the book will deal primarily with her own reactions to the McCarthy period and will not be a historical narrative: "It's [*Scoundrel Time*] mostly about me. I've tried to write about that ghastly period before, but this time I've forgotten about historical backgrounds and stuck to personal feelings, and I think it's worked out better" (Reed in Bryer 180). Few of her critics acknowledge what Hellman publicly stated in answer to the charge that her memoir is a "revisionist writing of the McCarthy era": "I don't think I rewrote history at all.... *Scoundrel Time* is about my personal experience before the House Un-American Committee [*sic*]. I wasn't out to write history. I was out to say this is what happened to me" (Rather in Bryer 212). The fury over *Scoundrel Time* and truth-value in autobiography can be traced to an obvious source: Hellman's forceful seizing of the right to promulgate her memory — "what happened to me" — as a valid version of history and resultant self-alignment with precepts that define Americanism.

The metaphors that Hellman uses in her memoirs to explain the workings of memory support the view that essential traits dictate the nature of the self and catalyze its evolution toward a finished state. The pervasiveness of the metaphors also unifies the volumes of her serial memoirs, thus strengthening the argument that each work should be studied in the context of the entire autobiographical project. These metaphors all suggest an unreachable but complete, integral memory that always just escapes her grasp. Further, the metaphors postulate a master text of unconscious memory to which she more easily gains access as she ages, an access that has confused readers looking for verifiable facts and chronological order. Her metaphors also reflect the interplay of the conscious and unconscious and delineate three distinct phases tracing how memory filters into her work. In her earliest phase, Hellman has relatively little control over access to memory; she seems baffled by its effect on her. In the second phase, she observes and acknowledges the emerging of unprompted memories from the unconscious. Toward the end of her life, as evidenced in *Maybe*, she no longer desires to control the mysterious processes of memory and surrenders to them.

In all of her memoirs except *Scoundrel Time*, Hellman refers to life and memory in terms of strands, fibers, ropes, or cords, metaphors through which she unfolds the three stages of her attitude toward memory. In describing the emotionally difficult period of her life when she was married to Arthur Kober and worked as a reader for a Hollywood studio, she suggests her lack of awareness about the consequences of her past: "I didn't even understand about my marriage, or my life, and had no knowledge of the new twists I was braiding into the kinks I was already bound round with" (*UW* 70). A retrospective and fatalistic view of this period of her life portrays life and memory as potentially strangling enterprises that trap her in their webs. Speaking of a much later stage of life, she also describes her relationship and memories of Dashiell Hammett as an "unfinished" braid: "the short cord that the years make into rope and, in my case, is there, hanging loose, long after death" (*UW* 298). Referring to Hammett literally as a loose end is fitting, since he remained figuratively present in Hellman's life after his death. This metaphor signifies the forever unresolved quality of their relationship. Despite Hammett's death, they continue to braid the bond begun nearly forty years before: "Even now, as I write this, I am still angry and amused that he always had to have things on his own terms: a few minutes ago I got up from the typewriter and railed against him for it, as if he could still hear me" (*UW* 297; parenthetical). Her reference in *Maybe* to life as "piles and bundles and ribbons and rags" (42) unravels the strangling braid she began unaware in the Hollywood days of her twenties and figuratively deconstructs the components that form the coherent, though unfinished, "cord" that keeps her attached to Hammett.

The numerous jungle metaphors indicate that Hellman feels overwhelmed with sorting out memories from/of the earlier stage of her life. In "Theatre," she describes the composition of *The Little Foxes*, the "most difficult" (*P* 473) play she ever wrote. Part of that difficulty she attributes to its "distant connection to [her] mother's family": "[E]verything that I had heard or seen or imagined had formed a giant tangled time-jungle in which I could find no space to walk without tripping over old roots, hearing old voices speak about histories made long before my day" (*P* 473–74). Early in her playwriting career, memories intrude and complicate her writing. Her past is an imprisoning net; vines obscure her vision and impede her freedom of movement. "Old voices speak" without her summons and force their "histories" onto her current project. At this point, she characterizes memory as an adversary with which she must struggle to proceed in her work.

Writing about the years during which she composed her memoirs, Hellman uses metaphors to suggest a significant change: that she no longer struggles with memory but trusts its ability to "offer up" what she needs to make necessary connections. She begins her portrait "Helen" by remarking on her lifelong fascination with "what lives in water and lies along its edges" (*UW* 249). Her realization in adulthood about what really fascinates her, "digging" in her unconscious, draws an interesting parallel with her other metaphor, pentimento—seeing what is beneath the surface of a painting. Water, like the aging surface of a painting, might be transparent or opaque, depending on the light, the angle of vision, or the time of viewing.

> One night about six months ago, when I was teaching at Harvard, it occurred to me that these childish, aimless pleasures — my knowledge of the sea has grown very little with time, and what interested me as a child still does — which have sometimes shamed me and often caused self-mocking, might have something to do with the digging about that occasionally happens when I am asleep. It is then that I awake, feeling that my head is made of sand and that a pole has just been pulled from it with the end of the pole carrying a card on which there is an answer to a long-forgotten problem, clearly solved and set out as if it had been arranged for me on a night table [*UW* 249–50].

In this instance Hellman is awakened in the middle of the night by a violent rainstorm and comes to a sudden, unprompted realization offered up by her unconscious "digging" in the sands of her memory: Helen and Sophronia (her housekeeper in the 1960s and her childhood nurse, respectively), "these two black women [she] loved more than [she] ever loved any other women," were "one person" to her (*UW* 250). Fragments of memory and information cohere for Hellman in this moment of awareness: finding a mangled watch on the beach two months before, remembering that she had bought the watch for Helen in the Zurich airport and that it had disappeared soon after she gave it to her, and realizing the events by which the watch came to be lost on the beach.

In *Maybe*, she again recounts an instance in which her unconscious performs its magic during sleep. After a night of heavy drinking, sleep, and subsequent sickness, disparate memories emanate from the "fog-banks" of Hellman's unconscious and provide answers: "I paid my [hotel] bill, got into the car and drove about five miles. It was not kindness that made me turn back. Something had stuck in my head through the fog-banks of the night before, something that had to do with me, something important I had missed" (33). While she sleeps, a truth emerges for Hellman from the master text of unconscious memory. Hellman comments in a 1979 addition to *Pentimento* that she wrote the entire book in a similar receptive state, a "weary semi-accuracy, a kind of 'free-association'" (*P* 586). Before writing each portrait in the book she "was waiting for ... what had some root that I had never traced before" (*P* 586). This remarkable receptivity contrasts with her struggle years earlier through "the giant tangled time-jungle" of memory.

The metaphors in *Maybe* illustrate Hellman's third stage, the acknowledgment that the process of remembering cannot be controlled or prompted at will. Although her metaphor of a "picture puzzle" suggests an unconscious master text of memory, she no longer attempts to assemble it. The metaphor of a puzzle with missing pieces dominates the book: "It's as if I have fitted parts of a picture puzzle and then a child overturned it and threw out some pieces" (51–52; passage in italics). Even though she has written the truth as she saw it (51), she realizes that mastering the autobiographical text is beyond her capability and even her desire. The text circles around the "missing pieces" only to reveal, finally, more about the nature of memory than about the characters who haunt Hellman. As Paul John Eakin puts it, "*Maybe* is also the story of story, the collapse of narrative as a structure of understanding" (*Touching* 226). Her fascination with the complexity of memory is most evident in *Scoundrel Time*'s complex subtexts and emendations.

Hellman achieves the "art of palimpsestic autobiography" in *Scoundrel Time* through subtexts that modify, elucidate, obscure, or transfigure the original version of her statement to HUAC (Adams 166). Through this method she embeds ideological reversals in the text. Her responses to aging, to the praise and attacks of her critics, and to her own re-evaluation of her work contribute to the reshaping of the text. *Scoundrel Time* lacks overt metaphors such as "pentimento" or "a tangle of jungle roots"; however, its subtexts, fluctuating emotional tone, and self-revising structure are evidence that Hellman emphasizes in it the same process of remembering that she emphasizes in the less "historical" works like *An Unfinished Woman*, *Pentimento*, and *Maybe*. In *An Unfinished Woman*, Hellman adopts a traditional narrative mode of autobiography, and seeks a "finished" self-portrait or unified self; in the palimpsestic *Pentimento*, she composes a self-portrait by examining herself from various perspectives — indirectly through portraits of other people (e.g., "Bethe" and "Julia") or a focus on a topic other than herself (e.g., "Theatre" or "'Turtle'").

Pentimento, a painter's term, means "'repented,' changed his mind"

(*P* 309), and corresponds on the textual level to the term palimpsest, although in the *act* of writing a palimpsest, both erasures and exposures of earlier texts occur. Through her subtexts and emendations, Hellman engages in a similar activity in *Scoundrel Time*. She repents, changes her mind, and embarks on the process of revising and re-evaluating her public image. Hellman defines the title *Pentimento* in the opening of the book: "Old paint on canvas, as it ages, sometimes becomes transparent. When that happens it is possible, in some pictures, to see the original lines: a tree will show through a woman's dress, a child makes way for a dog, a large boat is no longer on an open sea" (*P* 309). She implies a similarity between life and a canvas, or between human experience and a work of art. The transparency that sometimes results with the aging of the text and viewer allows one to see the subtext obscured by another text. With time, the memoir, Hellman's analogue to the painting, might allow her to see the past and present simultaneously — to join the "then" and "now" as Stein does at the close of *Everybody's Autobiography*. Hellman speculates, "Perhaps it would be as well to say that the old conception, replaced by a later choice, is a way of seeing and then seeing again" (309).

    The most obvious and potent palimpsestic technique in the text is the addition in 1979 of italicized subtexts to the original text. The italics demarcate a separate time frame and ideological position. All of her memoirs work backwards and forwards in time. They recross, revise, augment a core self, and generate a palimpsestic effect: "The figure of the palimpsest, of course, constitutes culture as we know it and is present in all writing, since writing repeats and erases, confirms and reverses, its own historical situation" (Benstock, *Left Bank* 351). All time frames and selves exist simultaneously in the text, overlapping, obscuring, highlighting, or contradicting previous imprints. Timothy Dow Adams argues that "Lillian Hellman's approach has been to thwart the process of identity formation deliberately. Instead of arriving at the end of the autobiographical act with the most current version of herself, she reverses the progression, beginning with an 'unfinished' self and ending with 'maybe,' moving, not toward a monument [James Olney's definition of autobiography as a 'monument of the self as it is becoming' (*Metaphor* 29)], but toward the destruction of a monument" (123). Hellman epitomizes the "process of integrating present selves with earlier selves [and] of aligning this synthesized self as it appears to the subject with the self that is recognized by others" (Shapiro 444). To redefine Shepard's term, her "galaxy" of selves comprises facets of the same woman, not Shepard's series of enigmatic identities masquerading under the same name and living in the same body. Nor is Hellman's ever self-revising "I" the absolutist, inviolable one created by Stein.

Scoundrel Time suspends itself between unfinished and finished and moves toward neither textual self-annihilation nor recovery of the theoretically complete self. In addition, her uncanny ability to see herself as a total stranger intensifies her objectification of her own life as if she were a fictional character. The year *Scoundrel Time* appeared, Hellman explained: "I try to write memoirs without being a central part of them" (Doudna in Bryer 201).[12]

Hellman conceives of the human being as a core self, an essential, unchangeable character that eventually surfaces, as do the original lines in pentimento or the erased texts in a palimpsest. Rather than fall prey to the past, she renews the self. As Katherine Lederer puts it, Hellman often mentions "her 'nature,' and the nature of other people," using the term in "an old-fashioned sense, as a description of traits formed early in life, stable and, consequently, knowable" (115–16).[13] In a diary entry dated one day prior to her appearance before the committee, she muses on the decisions of Clifford Odets and Elia Kazan to turn friendly witnesses and reveals her fatalistic belief in character in the old sense of the word: "It is impossible to think that a grown man, intelligent, doesn't have some sense of how he will act under pressure. It's all been decided so long ago, when you are very young, all mixed up with your childhood's definition of pride or dignity" (*ST* 664). She follows this fatalistic comment on character with a confident speculation that her own mettle will hold up under pressure: "I think this is why I don't like Joe's [her attorney, Joseph Rauh] occasional doubts about whether I will change my position once I am in the committee room; I may make an ass of myself, but that will be all" (*ST* 665). Rauh's "occasional doubts" made her uncomfortable because they challenged her belief in the solidity and triumph of character over circumstance. On the verge of her confrontation with the committee, she trusted, not mistakenly, that the soundness of her character had been firmly established long ago.

Along with palimpsestic techniques, Hellman effectively and deliberately uses subtexts to extend her power of authorship and to control her public image in post–Nixonian America. These subtexts express rhetorically Hellman's subjective concept of herself as an ever-revising but essential self. Among subtexts that extend her power to revise herself as a public commodity are the italicized additions to the 1979 reissue of *Scoundrel Time* in *Three*, the hypothetical versions of her statement to the committee, and the alternative versions of her letter to John Wood. *Scoundrel Time* shares a primary textual characteristic with her other three memoirs, *An Unfinished Woman*, *Pentimento*, and *Maybe, A Story*: its design generates a revision of her identity and ideological position. Various elements merge Hellman's past and present perspectives and continually resituate the text ideologically: the parenthetical comments that break the chronological narrative and mesh time frames, the diary excerpts, the bits of transcripts of the HUAC hearing, and the footnotes (e.g., on Whittaker Chambers).

The most significant of the subtexts in *Scoundrel Time* is the italicized section on rereading appended in 1979 in *Three*. This subtext extends her authorship and virtually unravels the text's emotional and ideological foundation. That she chose to reprint the original text intact, with the italicized section standing against or in response to the original text, emphasizes her tendency to layer ideological positions rather than deconstruct one before introducing another. She thus retains an unchanged core identity in this essential technique of extended authorship.

An intense need to control oneself as a commodity demands authoritative, continuing revision of one's public self, and Hellman shares with Stein and Shepard the compulsion to rewrite her autobiographical material over a period of years, sometimes recycling the same event in different texts. Upon rereading the "odd history" of *Scoundrel Time*, Hellman rejects the apparent coolness, calm, and tolerance she invented for the first edition. She admits to having "misrepresented" herself by appearing to be more emotionally controlled than she really was: "I wrote the book and I misrepresented myself in the book. I am, of course, sorry for that. I am not cool about those days, I am not tolerant about them and I never wish to be…. This book seemed to me last night too restrained" (725–26; passage in italics). Significantly, she avoids exploring the word "misrepresented." Had this word come from the pens of critics it might be construed as yet another damning accusation of intentional lying, yet she does not even address intent in her misrepresentation of herself. Instead, she revises the initial "calm" public image and inserts an "angry" public image that radically alters the emotional tone of the original text. Yet both positions stand. As her definition of *pentimento* explains, the "old conception" is replaced by a "later choice"; she sees and then sees again, imprinting one emotion over the other. One self bleeds through the image of another, introducing ambiguity and indeterminancy into self-definition.

Ironically, Hellman's original ending to *Scoundrel Time* undermines the message of her title. The closing lines of the original, "restrained" version of the text suggest an uncharacteristic mood of grateful acceptance, almost forgiveness: The scoundrel, time, in the end washes away the pain and anger of past injustices. Time has offered, however inadvertently, comfort, a kind of amnesia, and a mood of reconciliation reminiscent of Stein's closing lines in *Everybody's Autobiography*: "As I finish writing about this unpleasant part of my life, I tell myself that was then, and there is now,

and the years between then and now, and the then and now are one"
(*ST* 721). However, the phrase "unpleasant part" downplays the cataclysmic
effects of the McCarthy period on her private and professional life. Her
refuge in the commonsense philosophy that then was then and now is now
belies the rage evident in other sections of the text (e.g., her oft-cited attack
on the "intellectuals" of America who failed to speak up during the McCarthy
period [606]). Her choice to live "in the moment" to ameliorate the ravages
of time parallels Stein's resolution between identity and commitment to the
present in the last lines of *Everybody's Autobiography*: "[P]erhaps I am not
I even if my little dog knows me but anyway I like what I have and now it
is today" (318). For both authors, memory's ability to revise events, render
them less precise, and diffuse them into an achronological landscape becomes
an effective strategy to cope with an unpleasant past.

Her change from optimism to intense anger upon rereading her memoir in 1979 effects a dramatic emotional reversal in the text. In the earlier,
"restrained" version she is awed by her own emotion: "But I am angrier
now than I hope I will ever be again; more disturbed now than when it all
took place" (726; passage in italics). However, she also transforms that
anger into a positive force: "[T]he disasters of the McCarthy period were,
in many ways, good for me" (726; passage in italics). This fiery stand converts her memoir into a literary and moral triumph, despite the criticism
it received; furthermore, her position allows her to orchestrate a confrontation with the critics on her own terms, with Hellman departing ele-
gantly at its emotional crescendo.

Through another crucial subtext, her alternate version of the letter
to John Wood, Hellman continues the revision of public record and insists
on having her uncensored say years after the fact. (Hellman gave several
public versions of the alternate letter in interviews.) The "versions of the
statement [she] never made" (620) foreshadow the technique of extended
authorship she later exercises in *Scoundrel Time* by placing the 1979 subtext about rereading it in juxtaposition with the original text. What she
wanted to say officially to HUAC, but did not, looms as large as the actual
letter she sent and later published in *Scoundrel Time*:

> (But for five or six years after my appearance before the committee,
> when other troubles came, and I would be sleepless, I would get up at
> odd hours of the night and write versions of the statement I never
> made. I was certain that whatever would have been the injuries of jail
> they could not have been as bad as I had thought in those first days.
> Then, of course, when I had climbed back into bed to read a new and
> fancier version of what I hadn't said, I would think it's fine to do all

> this after the fears are over, you'd better cut it out and start worrying about how you will act when trouble comes again) [620–21].

Her revelation that alternate versions of the letter exist forces the reader of the 1970s to judge her not only on the basis of fact, but on what she would have *preferred* the facts to be and on emotions repressed for two decades. Through their emotional effect on the reader, these "versions of the statement" written in the "odd hours of the night" become part of American history and revise it by shifting her emotional and ideological position. For "five or six years" after her appearance before HUAC, Hellman experienced a disorientation in chronology; her confrontation with HUAC invaded her present, surfaced from her unconscious and repeatedly returned her to that pivotal moment.

Yet another subtext shifts the text's ideological ground: a hypothetical statement in which she expresses "the moral position for [her] taste" (620). She had refrained from this moral position at the 1952 hearing. However, by expressing it now, she invites the reader to evaluate her actions in light of what she *wishes* she could have done. She reverses the position she took in 1952 and proves wrong her prediction that she "would never be able to say it at all" (620).

> You are a bunch of headline seekers, using other people's lives for your own benefits. You know damn well that the people you've been calling before you never did much of anything, but you've browbeaten and bullied many of them into telling lies about sins they never committed. So go to hell and do what you want with me [620].

Clearly, Hellman's most damning criticism of the committee centers not only on its appropriation and control of the genuine memories of witnesses, but on its efforts to coerce the witnesses to fabricate memories that will consequently betray them. She accuses the committee of parasitically feeding off extorted memories from witnesses — the ultimate perversion of memory.[14] She explains the pathetic inventions conjured up by intimidated witnesses: "People were confessing to sins they'd never done; making up lies of meetings they'd been in when they'd been in no such meeting; asking God and the committee's pardon for nothing but just going into a room and listening to some rather dull talk" (Berger in Bryer 250). Hellman portrays herself in *Scoundrel Time* as anxious, terrified, and physically ill on the day of the hearing — as a witness who felt the best she could hope for would be to "come out unashamed" (668). But this belated "go to hell" command and the reality of what she did and *did not* do override that image and retroactively elevate her to the status of heroine. Like Stein, she invents herself as the supreme American, patriotic and moral in old-fashioned terms.

Dashiell Hammett's role in Hellman's construction of identity also demonstrates the power of her technique of extended authorship. She revises her text, her public image, American history, and shifts ideological positions. And as Hammett's case proves, she also revises and idealizes the public images of people essential to her own. In life and in death, Hammett functions as an extension of her, an icon that combines her moral code, reconstructed Americanism, and personal life.

Dashiell Hammett epitomized Hellman's belief in the endurance of character, and the moral constancy she attributes to him haunts the pages of *Scoundrel Time*. He was the icon against which she measured her sense of identity in her adult life, and he personified the American moral code through which she writes out her complex history. He was her political conscience, mentor, literary critic, lover, and friend — the "cool teacher" she intuitively sought. She writes of the confusing time before she met Hammett and her feeling of "going under": "I needed a teacher, a cool teacher, who would not be impressed or disturbed by a strange and difficult girl. I was to meet him, but not for another four or five years" (*UW* 63). Here, she reveals her search for an authority her fiercely independent nature could respect. Hellman also felt a profound professional debt to Hammett: "He taught me, in a sense, to write" (Adams in Bryer 225).[15] Her italicized comments in *Three* on rereading her 1966 portrait of Hammett sum up her absolutist vision of him and his effect on her moral outlook:

> When I met Hammett, who believed in neither ["right" nor "wrong"] but had formed a set of principles (and was to go on forming and revising them) by which he stood in eccentric isolation, I had come across what I needed. His rules were not my rules, but sometimes mine met his and we agreed, although that mattered less to me than Hammett's refusal to deviate from his, whatever the dangers or the temptations. I had found somebody who stood by himself, who was himself. For many people that would not be much to find: for me, even when I disagreed, it came at a time when I was going under [*UW* 304; passage in italics].

Hammett's "set of principles" and his "refusal to deviate" from them provided Hellman early in adulthood with a secular religion, a code by which to live. He defined *honor* for himself and "stuck with his rules" throughout his life (*UW* 281). Hammett's apparent sureness in his own sense of identity, his ability to stand by himself and be himself, saves Hellman at a dangerous and crucial point in her life.[16] Bernard Benstock observes that theirs was a symbiotic relationship (16), and he delineates its positive aspects: "What sustained their disjointed relationship was a mutual respect for each other's privacy and their diligence in never making unilateral decisions that incorporated the other. Theirs was a co-existence determined by their insistence on their distinct individualities, with agreed-upon dependencies and a delicate balance of shared concerns" (5). Carl Rollyson views Hammett as a pervasive "offstage presence" in Hellman's memoirs (392), and thinks that her "nature sought an anchor in Dashiell Hammett" (56). Rollyson's is the more typical view of the Hellman-Hammett relationship that stresses Hellman's dependence on Hammett more than the egalitarian and mutually supportive elements noted by Benstock.[17]

Clearly, Hellman did seek authority and structure in Hammett's committed, inflexible nature. Wagner-Martin argues that the key to the Hellman and Hammett relationship is "Hellman's looking for authority" and his "refusing" to be that authority ("Lillian Hellman" 281). Just as Sophronia was "the anchor for a little girl, the beloved of a young woman" (*UW* 251), Hammett was her anchor in adulthood.[18] In *Scoundrel Time* he plays the main role in her dramatization of herself as savior and American patriot and evolves into an icon of the patriotic American (rather ironic, given his legal battles over his supposedly un–American activities). In her eulogy to Hammett, she identifies him not with the America who imprisoned him for six months in 1951, but with the ideal America she and Hammett defined privately: "[H]e was a patriotic man, very involved in America" (Rollyson 391).

However, Hammett's admirable but inflexible moral stands also expressed themselves as dominance in a relationship that in other ways was mutually supportive. Repeatedly, Hellman emphasizes her dependence on his criticism of her writing, which she believes was given "without any malice" (171), although their writer-critic relationship, as she described it, sometimes exhibited characteristics that border on sado-masochism.[19] Hellman sums up the conflicting forces in their relationship in her portrait of Hammett in *An Unfinished Woman*. Even though he was the "most interesting man" she has ever met, she is angry that he "still interferes" with her in their imaginary conversations and "still dictates the rules" even from the grave (*UW* 299–300). Obviously, "his rules," which in her late twenties were "what [she] needed," become in later life a source of oppression for her (*UW* 304).

Ideologically speaking, however, Hammett was the political radical that she never had the "interest or commitment" to become (Moyers in Bryer

154). In 1976 Hellman's friend John Hersey wrote that Hammett had been and continued to be "her conscience" (26). Even upon first meeting Hammett, she intuited the essential difference in their characters: he was someone already committed at the time they met, and she "was never to be committed" (*UW* 133). But however central to her life and construction of identity Hammett was, he remained an enigma to Hellman, a fact that in itself was probably a main component in an attraction that lasted 31 years. To the question of "how a woman keeps a man interested in her for thirty years or how you really maintain a relationship like that without the conventional marriage as we know it," she responded, "I wish I knew that answer. I sure would try all over again" (Albert in Bryer 177). Three years after his death she refers to him as a "complex" man, and confesses that even she "knew so little of what he was" (Phillips and Hollander in Bryer 72). She attributes the intensity and longevity of their relationship to the silent communion so clearly a part of the "hours of the deer": "Without words, we knew that we had survived for the best of all reasons, the pleasure of each other" (*P* 501). Unwilling to be satisfied with Hellman's vague but sincere attempt to explain the attraction she and Hammett felt, Carl Rollyson explains the mysteriousness of their relationship with an unfortunate, clichéd image that fails to capture the complexity of their emotional and professional bond: "Hammett was the one man who forever eluded Lillian Hellman's grasp, the one man she most wanted to control and could not" (145).

The elaborate devices of emendations and subtexts make it difficult to evaluate the role of *Scoundrel Time* in Hellman's "recovery." Time has done little to lessen the emotional impact of the McCarthy period, even though she has reached an intellectual understanding of the events: "I recovered, maybe even more than that, in the sense of work and money. But I have to end this book almost as I began it: I have only in part recovered from the shock that came, as I guess most shocks do, from an unexamined belief that sprang from my own nature, time, and place. I had believed in intellectuals" (719). Thus, she comes full circle, ending the text as essentially the same woman who began it, disoriented and publicly betrayed by her absolutist faith in stable character traits and moral codes. Typically, however, the indomitable Hellman turns even this revelation of her disillusionment into a political and personal inspiration.

America: The Idea and the Ideal

The idealized Hammett and her own idealized, ever-revising self take center stage in *Scoundrel Time* as Hellman constructs and internalizes an ideal, more "real" America. Like Stein, she is at once the representative and the unique American. To align her code of "human decency" with America, Hellman exploits the doubleness of the memoir, its public and private faces, and conflates public and private truth, historical and personal narrative. In a somewhat circular argument, her Americanism gives her the license to interpret America and its recent history; she defends Americanism on this premise. Her Americanism, which she redefines as readily as she does *memoir*, connotes the most traditional of political views, not her infamous radical politics; thus her Americanism, like her palimpsest, layers rather than juxtaposes ideological positions.

Hellman's prophetic inner journey in *Scoundrel Time* attempts to counteract the corruption of America. This author of prophetic autobiography continues an American literary tradition by presenting herself as a "representative American self," whose "interpretation embod[ies] the only true America" (Bercovitch 186). "America" symbolizes Hellman's ideology, experiences, politics, and religious influences and combines them into one secular concept — human decency. *Scoundrel Time* documents what Mary G. Mason and Carol Hurd Greed call a "metaphorical journey," a journey with "a goal beyond the self," moving "toward involvement or commitment, to a creed, to an institution, to a leader, to another culture" (vii). This definition widens the interpretation of a traditional autobiographical experiential category and acknowledges the agency of woman, traditionally characterized as stasis and as obstacle to the spiritual and physical journeys of men.

The creative element in Hellman's homespun, traditional Americanism is her self-serving fluctuation between die-hard American individualism and collectivism, between individualist savior-dissenter and an ordinary citizen of collective America. Hellman conveniently and simultaneously takes refuge in the individual's right to dissent, and in the collective ideology based on conformity to a set of Puritan-derived values.[20]

Hellman, along with Stein, implies that her Americanism is the model against which the Americanism of others should be measured. Inflexible moral character is essential in resurrecting a declining America. In the role of individualist savior-dissenter, she traces her very right to refuse the committee's request to the "inherited right" of each American to rebel. She recognizes the sacred right to dissent in Dashiell Hammett's ability to take uncomplainingly his jail sentence in 1951 for "refusing to give the names of the contributors to the bail bond fund of the Civil Rights Congress" (614):

> He had known that if you differ from society, no matter how many
> pieties they talk they will punish you for disturbing them. No such

> thing had ever occurred to me; when I disagreed I was exercising my
> inherited rights, and certainly there could be no punishment for doing
> what I had been taught to do by teachers, books, American history.
> It was not only my right, it was my duty to speak or act against what
> I thought was wrong or dangerous [615].

Paradoxically, her individuality originates in conformity to Americanism
(that is, individuality leads to collective identity); she rebels in the names
of patriotism and duty and upholds her staunch belief in "American character." Founding her Americanism on childhood memories and American
history, she distills it to the pure act of exercising her duty to speak out
against injustice. Here, Hellman differentiates between "society," the
imperfect America that persecutes people like Hammett, and the ideal
America inculcated in the minds of school children and constructed in history books. Despite evidence that the ideal America would never supplant
the unjust society, Hellman remains dedicated to the America taught by
"teachers, books, [and] American history." Hellman's unabashed, simplistic idea of Americanism, as she defined it at the time of her 1952 appearance before HUAC, rivals Stein's in its seeming naiveté.

   Scoundrel Time includes a political agenda; it provides a blueprint for
the resurgence of an Americanism under threat by the likes of McCarthy
and Nixon. Hellman's moralism answers the America that "cries out for
belief" and "has none" (679). She traces her unshakable belief in character as far back as her adolescence and notes that during the period covered in the portrait "Bethe" (early adolescence), she was in her "high-class
moral theory stage from which I have never completely emerged" (*UW*
338). Hellman was frequently dismissed as a "moralist" for her genuine
concern for her country, but her friend John Hersey took a different view
of her leadership in 1976 when he called her a "moral force," and "almost
an institution of conscience for the rest of us" (25). Alluding to what Hellman called her "Puritan conscience" (*UW* 63), he feels that her "stern code
touches the national nerve at just the right moment" in a nation suffering
from Nixonism (27). Hammett called this attitude her "honor child stuff"
(710), and it resurfaces throughout her memoirs and interviews and was
noted by herself and others. Hammett labeled her "Miss Religious L. H."
on a sign marking the grave of the title character of "Turtle" (a turtle that
was supposed to become turtle soup but was eventually killed and buried
by Hellman) (*P* 585). He also thought her "the only Jew he knew who was
also a Puritan" (Reed in Bryer 183). Oddly enough, though she credited
Hammett with an inflexible sense of right and wrong, she recalls in her
1979 italicized addition to the Hammett portrait that he told her that it

was she, not he, who had "*the rigid ideas of right and wrong*" (*UW* 303; italicized). Even Joseph Rauh characterized her as "a Puritan Lady" (648).

Under pressure, Hellman admitted that she had a religious nature, although she was uncomfortable with the fact. She tells a friend during her visit to Russia in the 1960s, "Well, I'm religious, I guess, although I don't like to think that. So I told myself then that if they didn't put Hammett back in jail, if he could be sick and die in peace, I would be a good girl, like a nun, and not ask for anything else" (*UW* 228).

Hellman's role as moralist/heroine is all the more interesting and complex because she undermines it as she constructs it. She adopts in *Scoundrel Time* what Bernard Benstock calls "a self-congratulatory tone" (7). But in *Scoundrel Time* she also indicts herself for cowardice, echoing her statement about how easy it is to write alternate letters to HUAC once the threat is over: "Many people have said they liked what I did, but I don't much, and if I hadn't worried about rats in jail, and such ... Ah, the bravery you tell yourself was possible when it's all over, the bravery of the staircase" (676). To be fair, Hellman does do with pride and conviction exactly what Sidney Hook accused her of — she "pictures herself as a heroine defending intellectual and cultural freedom against her inquisitors" (86).

Writing in the wake of Watergate, she more than once points out the parallels between McCarthyism and Nixonism in hope of rescuing America from its fallen state. Watergate, by her logic, is a mere extension of the McCarthy period. She discerns an Orwellian connection between the imprecise language used in both periods to confuse and manipulate an undiscerning public. She parallels the gullibility of the American public regarding the "double-talk we were to hear in the Watergate days," and the public's tacit agreement in the fifties "to swallow any nonsense that was repeated often enough, without examination of its meaning or investigation into its roots" (644).

In a particularly damning comment, she implies that America's tendency toward boredom, its short attention span, and its failure to remember contribute to the repetition of political and moral disasters such as the McCarthy period and Watergate. Interestingly, she assumes a double role: the savior-dissenter "I" who diagnoses America's ills and the "we," the American population who were not "shocked," "surprised," or "angered," but merely "bored" with Joe McCarthy and his "cheap baddies" (604).

> The editor and critic Philip Rahv, an early anti–Communist and then an early anti-anti-Communist, had said it a year before in one of his least decipherable growls: "Nothing can last in America more than ten

> years. McCarthy will soon be finished." And that, I think, was the
> truth, just that and not much more. We were not shocked at the dam-
> age McCarthy had done, or the ruin he had brought on many people.
> Nor had we been surprised or angered by Cohn and Schine playing
> with the law as if it were a batch of fudge they enjoyed after the plea-
> sure of their nightly pillow fight. We were bored with them. That and
> nothing more [717].

A maximum attention span of ten years dooms America to repeated bouts
of moral upheaval, Hellman warns. Our failure to remember makes us
victims of history; our rejection of continuity (and therefore history) condemns us. Uncommitted to a moral code, she asserts, the nation drowns
in a "relativistic morality" (de Pue in Bryer 190), which robs us of our historical context and plunges us into what Shepard calls "chaos." Lacking
an absolutist moral code and memory, traits that Hellman adamantly
claims for herself in *Scoundrel Time*, the America of the 1970s in no way
resembles the fictional America Hellman espouses as ideology.

In a 1958 interview, only six years after her appearance before HUAC,
she signals her increasing alarm over the passive, distracted state of the
American people. An insidious, pervasive consumerism and sloganism
engulfs 1950s' America, she warns. The nation has been through a period
of "childish self-deception," avoiding the problems confronting it by losing itself in nationalistic materialism. We Americans, Hellman feels,
"wanted to think of ourselves as the best and kindest and most generous
and most moral and most middle-class and most split-level and most wall-
to-wall carpeting people that ever existed, and anything that intruded on
that ..." (Stern in Bryer 37).

As caretaker of America's morality, Hellman believes that "conscience
includes the fate of other people" and extends beyond mere "personal salvation" (Doudna in Bryer 203). During the 1960s that attitude was most
evident in her messages to American youth. In the true prophetic mode,
she charges American youth with the responsibility of America's destiny.
Citing the early Christian and Jewish religions as examples of "great move-
ments" that have a conscience, she makes a connection between traditional
religious codes and her secular "human decency" (Doudna in Bryer 203).
Her comparison of the sixties generation with the youth involved in the
Spanish Civil War presents a striking example of how her palimpsestic text
conflates time frames and political ideologies. As late as 1968 she attributed a "solid idealism" to young people (Gardner in Bryer 120).

Her prophetic tone intensifies in her 1975 commencement address to
Barnard College (printed in *Mademoiselle*'s college edition). In a typical
Steinian tactic, she adopts the anonymous collective voice to propagate

highly personal views. Lamenting the "calm, pleasant, well-mannered shrugging acceptance of life in America" prevalent in 1975, she urges the graduates not to succumb to the powerlessness that has made most Americans no longer able to believe "that government was ever intended to belong to us." Situating her audience historically, she informs them that they have lived through "the most shocking period of American history." She was explicit: "You have seen a White House disgraced. You have heard a president of your country lie over and over again to you. You have seen a pious-talking vice president thrown out because he was a crook." Tracing America's "lack of belief" to the post–Vietnam War period and the height of student protest, she catalogues the sins of the C.I.A., the F.B.I., and other government agencies during the Watergate era. Those sins include "possibly ... murder, or plots to murder." Dramatically stating, "We didn't think of ourselves that way once upon a time," she closes her address with a plea to American youth to accept their "absolute duty" and "to put an end to all that." In essence, she implores them to believe in and resurrect her ideal, privately envisioned America.

However, by the writing of *Scoundrel Time* her hope that the youth of America would close the gap between the real and ideal had greatly diminished. The 1979 italicized additions to her chapter on Spain and the Spanish Civil War in *An Unfinished Woman* credit the present American generation with aspirations to the idealism of the Spanish Brigades, but she also points out their inability to achieve it: "That must, has to be, a very pure state of being and I think the cleanness and clarity of it is what the present generation recognizes, envies, or wants for itself" (129). Near the close of *Scoundrel Time*, she sarcastically expresses her disappointment in "the good children of the Sixties" (719), from whom she expected so much. Only four years after her Barnard address, her optimism about the youth of America has become cynicism, and she pessimistically predicts that America's youth "are well on their way to a sort of shoulder-shrugging conservatism" (723). The one hope for America's youth, she believes, is that "they do not have much knowledge of fear" (723). This crucial "lack of fear" (724), a trait she admired in Hammett and the deer at the farm, may be the salvation of America, the only way to rejuvenate "another," earlier America based on the right to dissent, a Western cultural tradition: "[T]his lack of fear has its roots in another America and maybe in eighteenth-century France or England, or wherever men of the Western world were early insisting upon freedom for dissident political opinion" (724). Ultimately she is left, like the loner and individualist Hammett, with her American dream and ideals. But she was never silent.

Hellman's premise that "after all, writing is the process of making use of yourself or what you come out with from other people" (Funke in Bryer 97) gives her license to reinvent or manipulate the autobiographical genre, especially since she insists, in a typical evasive and strategic move, that she "wasn't out to write history. I was out to say this is what happened to me" (Rather in Bryer 212). But the argument will continue over the value of *Scoundrel Time* as a historical document — indeed, over its *obligation* to be one — and its failure to reaffirm Nixonian America's self-image as endorsed by the 1970s' version of history.

It is time to stop viewing *Scoundrel Time* solely as revisionist American history, to examine it, instead, with as much respect for the subjective nature of autobiography as Hellman herself had when she exploited the doubleness of the memoir. Despite the fact that *Scoundrel Time* deals largely with verifiable, "factual" American history, it is a text with as many layers and revisions as her palimpsestic memoir *Pentimento*. In *Scoundrel Time*, Hellman continues the concepts of a self-revising identity, an ever-evolving core self that eventually encompasses all the women Hellman has been or ever wanted to be and that constitutes a layered portrait explained by her use of the term *pentimento*. Among the most crucial and decentering of the subtexts through which she exercises ownership of memory and extended authorship are the alternate statements she could have made before HUAC but did not and her 1979 italicized emendations upon rereading *Scoundrel Time* (as published in *Three*). The text remains an open forum for her involvement in the McCarthy period. The extended authorship Hellman exercises in her controversial memoir through subtexts and emendations maintains control over her public image and continues to dictate public reaction years after the text's initial publication. Thus, she easily encompasses a continuum of often contradictory ideological positions.

Scoundrel Time is about loss — of place, of political idealism, of a way of life, and of financial stability, things that spelled an ideal American existence for Hellman. But it reinterprets and optimistically transforms loss into a moral lesson. Thus, like Stein, Hellman reconciles herself to the past and frees herself from the scoundrel time and closes the 1979 edition of *Scoundrel Time* with a final flippant and angry comment on the entire McCarthy fiasco: "*And to hell with the fancy reasons they give for what they did*" (726; italicized). Hellman's initial reluctance to write about the McCarthy period derives from a temporary inability to talk about it, not from amnesia or a gap in memory. Although Hellman professes emotional detachment and freedom from the past, she betrays her fascination with the past simply by writing *Scoundrel Time*. But most important, she demonstrates her personal strength by facing the past and attempting to revitalize the America that stands for character, "decency," and political activism. Her authoritative seizing of the past precludes the permanent sense of emotional loss that haunts Stein and Shepard in their contemplation of the past and suggests the empowerment possible by conjoining the personal and political. Her resiliency emerges in this optimistic assessment of the year or so following the HUAC appearance: "I was learning that change, loss, an altered life, is only a danger when you become devoted to disaster" (700).

Scoundrel Time is her successful and fiery fight for memory on her own terms; and whether or not we accept the text as a form of revisionist history, we must acknowledge that Hellman literally fought to the death (whether wise or not) to claim her memory as a repository of American history as valid as anyone else's.[21] That conviction to remember also takes on an idealistic tone, for her memoirs record her lengthy and violent confrontation with the scoundrel time, a metaphor for the insidious moral and political conditions of America in the 1950s, 1960s, and 1970s, not her urge to avoid the confrontation. Accomplishing her early dictum that all writing should be propaganda in this ambiguously labeled memoir, she transforms her political radicalism into simple "human decency," a nostalgic longing for a lost America — if indeed that place ever existed — and refuses to be restricted by generic tradition or public opinion.

CHAPTER FOUR

Sam Shepard's
Motel Chronicles:
A Microcosmic America

The epigraph to *Motel Chronicles*, "never did far away charge so close," a quotation from Peruvian poet Cesar Vallejo, sets a precedent for conceiving of memory in terms of space, territory, or geographical proximity or distance. As a textual map, *Motel Chronicles* reinforces the equivalence between memory and geography and registers Shepard's displaced relationship with America and the self. The very title *Motel Chronicles* links wandering and displacement with writing. An American invention, the *motel*, epitomizes the American tendencies toward movement, expansion, and the creation of temporary place; *chronicles*, in a historical sense, inscribes that wandering in time and place. Shepard's autobiographical act responds to and extends the legacy descended from the days of the American frontier, through Whitman, and culminating in Kerouac; *Motel Chronicles* is a version of America "on the road," a migratory experience rather than a stable geographical place.

Shepard foregrounds ruptures and contradictions in the weave of the unitary autobiographical self that undermine his efforts to constitute an America. The instability and fragmentation in the tangle of the divided self are emphasized by these contradictions: his simultaneous and equally intense spiritual attachment to the land and to freedom and mobility; his longing for the stability offered by the context of American history and culture and the need to escape it; the lament over his inevitable emotional "separateness" and his desire for aloneness; his longing for the father and the rejection of the father's world; his desire to recapture the blissful union with the mother and the urge to abandon it; and the recognition of the American frontier and the West as a historical and tangible reality as well as — in truth — purely a state of mind.[1] Converted into landmarks of Shepard's memory, America becomes his medium for self-definition, but ultimately fails to reflect a unified self implied by the authorial signature.

Shepard wrote the text during a time of emotional crisis when he openly questioned the stability and nature of identity. Soon after finishing *Motel Chronicles* (November 1982), Shepard separated from his wife O-Lan Johnson and his child Jesse Mojo and began to live with actor and movie producer Jessica Lange. He writes to friend and collaborator Joseph Chaikin on August 3, 1983: "I'm still in a strange time of transition. This whole change has been full of all kinds of powerful emotions from the most violent to the most tender. I feel very exhausted from it all and at the same time exhilarated. It's as though I was swept up in a hurricane and landed in a foreign land" (Daniels 120). In a letter written less than a year after finishing the book, he clarifies the stresses and contradictions so visible in *Motel Chronicles*:

> Something's been coming to me lately about this whole question of being *lost*. It only makes sense to me in relation to an idea of one's identity being shattered under severe personal circumstances — in a state of crisis where everything that I've previously identified with in myself suddenly falls away…. [T]he resulting emptiness or aloneness is what interests me. Particularly to do with questions like *home*? *family*? the identification of *others* over time? people I've known who are now lost to me even though still alive? trying to track someone down from long ago in my past — someone I knew *then* but now have no idea who they might be. A living ghost hunting now in the present for a life that is always escaping [Daniels 128–29].

This passage captures several important issues in the text: Shepard's focus on individual and collective identity — particularly as reflected in his ambivalence about family; the impermanence and plurality of identity; the potential loss of identity rising from that impermanence, as in Scarlett Johnson's (Shepard's mother-in-law) loss of memory after a brain hemorrhage in 1979; and the displacement that robs one of home.

The letter suggests that Shepard drastically revised his concept of identity during this emotionally stressful time. His familiar identity "shatter[s]" and "fall[s] away," signaling a rebirth. He writes "in a state of crisis," intrigued by the contrast between his "aloneness" and the collective, stabilized identities of "others" that culminate "over time" and are inter-dependent with his own identity. His self-characterization as "a living ghost" stresses his emptied-out state, his loss of a sense of self. While Shepard remains enmeshed in his aloneness and feeling of having lost his identity, life escapes him. The components of life no longer form a coher-ent narrative. Like Hellman, he senses that the randomness of events pre-vents him from believing in that narrative.

Shepard does not respond to the fiction of the unitary self with Stein-ian anxiety, however, but with a challenging view of identity based on that very disunity. Unlike Stein, he does not give birth to the self by con-structing a monolithic identity that absorbs, incorporates, or co-opts America and binds the splits between private and public selves. His pro-ject is not to prevent but to experience and record the "shattering" of his identity; thus, he seeks psychological assurance in the very condition Stein avoids. His autobiographical work reflects the ideal entity of his dramatic works, as described in his correspondence to Joseph Chaikin: "the char-acterless character" (Daniels 123), "a kind of lost soul hunting through various attitudes and inner lives for a suitable 'character'" (Daniels 123), or an "actor playing multiple characters" (Daniels 128). Shepard's com-ment to Ben Brantley focuses on the emptied-out feeling that Shepard aims for in writing, acting, and directing — a condition all the more complex because it releases "multitudes" of shifting identities (Schiff): "To me, a strong sense of self isn't believing in a lot. Some people might define it that way, saying, 'He has a very strong sense of himself.' But it's a complete lie" (26H).

Shepard disperses the narrative authority of *Motel Chronicles* with a range of evasive pronoun positions to achieve this plural identity of "var-ious attitudes and inner lives." His plural identity reverses the child's assumption of its "allotted place in the Symbolic Order" and instead refuses to give up "the claim to imaginary identity with all other possible posi-tions" (Moi 99). There is no sense that Shepard nurtures or seeks, as does Hellman, to preserve an essential, more authentic self in opposition to this interplay of identities.

Motel Chronicles is a most significant autobiographical work in that it exhibits what Michael Sprinker deems "a pervasive and unsettling fea-ture in modern culture — the gradual metamorphosis of an individual with a distinct, personal identity into a sign, a cipher, an image no longer clearly and positively identifiable as 'this one person'" (322). Shepard releases what he calls "the galaxies inside of us," the multiple selves inside the "social person that we present to each other" (Lippman 12), and records the exploration of his shattered identity.

Thus, America is an internal map on which Shepard projects his displacement and with which he re-orients himself. Shepard's short account of finding "a dead water-bird in the middle of a parking lot" (67) defines the displacement prevalent in *Motel Chronicles*—a condition in which our intuitive and even our physical faculties fail to orient us in the world:

> I found a dead water-bird in the middle of a parking lot. There were no cars. The bird was in perfect condition. Still limp and not a sign of blood. I brought the bird home and stuck it in the ice box. The next day me and my Dad took it around the neighborhood asking people if they'd ever seen a bird like that before. Nobody had. We took it to a Taxidermist and he couldn't tell what kind of bird it was either, although we all agreed it must be a water-bird because it had webbed feet [67].

He, his father, and a taxidermist formulate a theory that "the bird was flying over the parking lot and mistook the reflection off the pavement for a lake" (67). Shepard identifies with the bird and is haunted by his belief that the bird was betrayed by its own instincts: "I kept putting myself in the bird's place, flying high above the parking lot, cruising for a lake. Why would a bird like that be so far from where lakes were to begin with? How could a bird get lost?" (67). What insidious disorder has led even nature astray? A note of desperation enters as he ponders the mystery of the bird with a broken neck, otherwise in perfect condition. What hope is there for human beings when even birds, whose internal radar guides them thousands of miles in migration, get lost and die because they cannot orient themselves?

Shepard's identification with the "bird's place" represents in microcosm the central issue in *Motel Chronicles*: the mystery and confusion arising from Shepard's own physical and mental displacement and disorientation.[2] The text both glorifies and counteracts the syndrome of "on the road." For Shepard, writing embodies a "deep connection" (72) and a "stillness" (121); it provides orientation and placement in the midst of alienation. He responds to displacement by making a home for himself on paper; as with Stein, the act of writing becomes primary.

Oddly, Shepard links displacement and mental disorientation with a spiritual purpose in his comment on the Rolling Thunder Revue[3]: "What is this whole thing about? Is it a spiritual sojourn of some kind? Just another rock tour? What in the fuck are we doing out here in blind America looking for a hotel room?... The past is this moment escaping" (*RTL* 45). Shepard's displacement resembles the condition of "placelessness," a geography Edward Relph characterizes as a "labyrinth of endless similarities," a condition that "cuts roots, erodes symbols, and replaces diversity with uniformity and experiential order with conceptual order" (141, 143). Placelessness homogenizes and diminishes place.[4]

But, significantly, Shepard continually transforms, in the tradition of Walt Whitman, the negative aspects of American mobility and detachment from the land into a positive assessment of being "on the road."[5] Shepard's re-orientation paradoxically encompasses both movement and stillness. The road is itself the destination.[6] Shepard, along with many other American writers (such as Jack Kerouac and Joan Didion), identifies the highway as the personification of twentieth-century placelessness. The highway epitomizes Shepard's and Americans' simultaneous attachment to the land and desire for mobility. The highway, "a universal place like space" (Lutwack 227), exists only to be traversed. America's identity as an ever-expanding frontier of white culture culminates in Kerouac's obsession with crossing and recrossing the continent. The endless deferring of America's identity, predicated on migration and the dream of reaching some as yet unexperienced land, parallels Shepard's search for an endless cast of undiscovered selves.

In *Motel Chronicles*, the vast geography of America symbolizes a private geography in which Shepard differentiates between two types of place, which can be called, respectively, place and space, roughly equivalent to physical and mental geography. Place for Shepard is a physical location, and space an absence of place, or a state-of-mind. Human content imbues place, and human purpose contaminates it. Place is "inhabitable space" (Lutwack 27), usually urban; it is the house filled with family that he "wonder[s] about leaving" (*MC* 124) or "Poor Texas / Carved into / like all the rest" with the contamination of Holiday Inns and swimming pools (26). It corresponds to a tangible, geographical reality — a house bustling with family; Los Angeles, where people "become / the people / they're pretending to be" (42); or the apartment in which he last remembers seeing his friend (73). Space, however, corresponds to a mental geography, such as an open field halfway between San Francisco and Los Angeles. Space is the equivalent of Stein's "entity" or Hellman's idealized "hours of the deer," in which self and place coalesce. The tyranny of the father's name does not taint space or "stillness." Stillness is the antithesis of physical and mental activity: "The Pasture is soaked in rain. I don't feel like moving much. I'd just as soon live in this truck. I'd just as soon let the grass grow right through the tires" (58). Shepard repeatedly associates absence of thought, empty space, and spatial and temporal dislocation with freedom:

is it a motel room
or someone's house

is it the body of me alive
or dead

is it Texas
or West Berlin

what time is it
anyway

what thoughts
can I call allies

I pray for a break
from all thought
a clean break
in blank space
let me hit the road
empty-headed [20].

The speaker voices the disorientation and displacement he feels both geographically — "is it Texas / or West Berlin" — and within his own body: "is it the body of me alive / or dead." This decentered state propels him toward a place not definable in geographical or chronological terms. The time of day seems irrelevant, as does whether he is in a motel room in West Berlin or in a house in Texas. Refuge lies in a "blank space" where time, geography, and identity do not matter. Even thoughts must be banished from the pristine space he wants to reach. In a "clean break" he can even abandon thinking and "hit the road / empty-headed." With disorientation as the impetus, the experience of displacement transforms into a spiritual release — a re-orientation to place. "Hit[ting] the road" or displacement itself becomes his destination; "on the road" becomes a positive mode of existence.

Shepard's place of spiritual revitalization takes the geographical form of frontier or the West (what critics often call "Shepard country"). Shepard internalizes the American frontier, for him a spiritualized space free of human activity more than a place of mountains, desert, sky, and plains. The American West stands for freedom from the very culture that defines it. Shepard projects his Edenic spiritualized frontier onto America's real[7] geography and transforms the frontier into "stillness of space" (121). In *Angel City*, the West is a place of introspection — the "Looks-Within" place (*FFL* 97). His relationship to landscape supports Relph's assertion that for some people, "a profound attachment to place is as necessary and significant as a close relationship with other people" (Preface). In *Motel Chronicles,* Shepard achieves an intimacy with the American landscape that he finds difficult to establish in human relationships.

An area "always the same ... always the borderline" (Wilson 148), the West or frontier constitutes not so much a place in itself as it constitutes the demarcation or seam between places. The frontier is a "place without history because it remains unchanging" (Wilson 148), its identity and function as a boundary remaining constant wherever it is physically located. In Shepard's view, the American West offers "the hope of redemption" and freedom from the "confinements of civilization" (Wetzsteon 260). Bonnie Marranca notes that in *True West* (in *Seven Plays*), for example, the desert, a landscape of empty space that is devoid of features that humanize or civilize place, symbolizes salvation ("Alphabetical" 17). In *Motel Chronicles,* as well as *True West, Curse of the Starving Class,* and other Shepard works, the anti-social father retreats to the desert to find peace within himself and to avoid confronting a civilization intent on homogenizing the individual spirit so that it will conform to society.

Shepard's desire to unite spiritually with the landscape and to escape the strait-jacket of identity manifests itself as *topophilia,* "a peak experience" or "ecstatic experience of pure individuality and identity that stems from some encounter with place" (Relph 37). Repeatedly in *Motel Chronicles,* he returns to the intimate "connection" with the land that transcends the land itself: "it's true / this deep connection / it's really true / the earth gives off a message / it breathes out / I catch it on the inhale / skunks / dead rabbits / the day's heat escapes" (72). Shepard's recurring word "true" stresses the authenticity of the experience. He literally inhales the earth's exhale in a symbiotic breathing process.

In a third-person narrative about a nighttime truck ride, the character visualizes an out-of-body spiritual experience during transcendent moments in a dark field. "He" stops halfway between San Francisco and Los Angeles, crawls under a barbed-wire fence and sits "cross-legged in the middle of [the Harris Feedlot]" (121). As "the raw smell of cattle fill[s] his chest" (121), he desires "nothing but stillness" (121). The smells and feel of the land eradicate place and identity:

> A huge hand grabbed him from behind. A hand without a body. It carried him up, miles above the highway. He didn't fight. He'd lost the fear of falling. The hand went straight through his back and grabbed his heart. It didn't squeeze. It was a grip of pure love. He let his body drop and watched it tumble without hope. His heart stayed high, tucked in the knuckles of a giant fist [121].

The state of solitude and "stillness" replaces the landscape as a tangible place. From a superior perspective, "he" [Shepard] experiences a loss of fear in the completeness of "pure love."

Even his description of his geographical location reflects a transcendent perspective:

> Suspended. Tiny San Francisco dangling to the north: innocent, rich and a little bit silly. The sprawling, demented snake of L.A. to the south. Its fanged mouth wide open, eyes blazing, paralyzed in a lunge of pure paranoia. This was the place to be, he thought. Right here. In the middle. Smack in the belly of California where he could eyeball both from a distance. He could live inside the intestines of this valley while he spied on the brain and the genitals [121].

He designs a map of California only loosely based on geographical reality. Situating himself in the "belly" or center — on the frontier between the cities contaminated by human vices — he voyeuristically communes with the entire spirit of California without commitment to the intellect ("brain") or the physical ("genitals"); he escapes altogether the burden of the physical body as when "a grip of pure love" releases his body: "He let his body drop and watched it tumble without hope." Geographical "distance" translates into psychological distance; from the vantage point of the "intestines of [the] valley" he views his dichotomized self. His body and heart separate, the heart surrendering to a "hand without a body." His transcendent self, identified with "pure love," abandons the body and watches it fall away.

That the American West also poses a threat in addition to offering spiritual release problematizes Shepard's equating the frontier and open spaces with freedom. Disassociated from history, the frontier also represents the "terror" of the failure to identify oneself with history.[8] In an interview in the 1970s during his residence in England, Shepard identifies America itself as a place lacking the stabilizing effects of history and acknowledges the devastating effect of that condition on the human psyche: "One of the weird things about being in America now, though I haven't been there much lately, is that you don't have any connection with the past, with what history means. And then you've got this emotional thing that goes a long way back, which creates a certain kind of chaos, a kind of terror" ("Metaphors" 196). The stabilizing effects of history, or collective identity, can never be reconciled with the inherent emotional "chaos" that we each inherit. At times, Shepard seeks escape from the "connection with the past" and its tyrannical power to determine the present. However, in this interview, he parallels Hellman in embracing history and envisioning it as personal and collective salvation.

A map itself is history, a culminating record of humankind's division of the land and the establishment of national identity boundaries — the human race's evolving process of identity formation. A map projects on a grand scale humankind's desire to make a home, to re-orient, and to legitimize geographical entities by endowing them with proper names — a process that mirrors an author's autobiographical objectives. Shepard points out the human drive to "make connections" with the earth and other people. Maps project those needs onto a visual model that ensures us against the vertigo of cultural and emotional displacement — the "chaos" and "terror" Shepard finds inherent in the human condition. Through the textual map of *Motel Chronicles*, Shepard examines and rebinds himself to the terror of his personal history and faces his ambivalent emotions about family and individual identity, "home" and mobility, history's simultaneous threat and comfort, mother and father, and separateness and mergence. He re-orients the displaced selves that live in his memory and his text.

Separation and Mergence: Paternal and Maternal

Shepard's strong sense of the divided and alienated self which he addresses in his plays took physical form in his four years expatriation in England and Nova Scotia, which gave him the exile's "heightened consciousness of the physical and social environment" (Kennedy, "Place" 515). Shepard parallels Stein in consciously seeking a definition of America and Americanism through expatriation. In his own words, by living in England he "found out what it really means to be an American" ("Metaphors" 198).[9] To define oneself as an American one must face the inescapable consequences of the cultural past: "The more distant you are from it [America], the more the implications of what you grew up with start to emerge" (198). For both Stein and Shepard, expatriation resulted in a rebinding of selfhood and Americanism. But Shepard does not become, as did Stein, the self-defined monolith against which America and American culture define themselves. He constructs and knows the self by situating himself in the larger context of family, culture, and nation. He, in contrast to Stein, acknowledges origins, influences, biases, and limitations.

The self-division Shepard expresses so explicitly in geographical terms as he defines expatriation also manifests itself in the conflicts between his individual and familial/collective identities, and between the paternal and maternal worlds. Changing his legal name in 1963 after a serious fight with his father demonstrates his ambivalence toward family, on both a personal and institutional level. Shepard's break with the father is synonymous with his rejection of the family as an institution and of his intention to forge an independent identity: "There was this big fight with my old man, and at that point I fled. And I thought, well, I'm just going to have to start over, pretend I don't even have a family" (Kroll 70). Shepard's own name was handed down "through seven generations of men with the same name each naming the first son the same name as the father."[10] Born Sam Shepard Rogers, Jr., he was called Steve. The irony of the name change did not reveal itself to Shepard immediately: "Years later, I found out that Steve Rogers was the original name of Captain America in the comics" (Shewey, *Sam Shepard* 31). Turning away from the family structure signaled for him a turn to America's art, pop culture, and mythology for meaning.

Shepard's discourse on the patronymic and nicknames epitomizes the opposition of the mother's and the father's worlds and also reveals his simultaneous rejection of and longing for his father:

> My name came down through seven generations of men with the same name each naming the first son the same name as the father then the mothers nicknaming the sons so as not to confuse them with the fathers when hearing their names called in the open air while working side by side in the waist-high wheat.
>
> The sons came to believe their names were the nicknames they heard floating across these fields and answered to these names building ideas of who they were around the sound never dreaming their real legal name was lying in wait for them written on some paper in Chicago and that name would be the name they'd prefix with "Mr." and that name would be the name they'd die with [49].

The lineage of the "real legal name" perpetuates the father's world. The name from the father is the name you "die with." This denial of that bond resembles Stein's rejection of the dead grandmother's *G*; the institutionalized family names compromise subjective identity. However, the nickname the mother gives the son differentiates him from the father and endows the child with a separate identity. The son comes to believe that the nickname "heard floating across ... fields" is his actual name. While the sons were "building ideas of who they were around the sound" of the nickname, the legitimate identity, like a snake, was "lying in wait for them" in legal records in Chicago. The name of the father offers a world of succession, the name being a preassigned, stable identity to which one is bound even before associating the sound of the name with oneself. The nickname given by the mother represents an identity of possibility and freedom; the sons "answer" to the illegitimate names given by the mothers because the nicknames recognize the autonomy of the sons, their right to "build" their own identities. The nickname is not just a death sentence to "prefix with 'Mr.,'" but an invitation to shape one's own birth and life to the "sound" of the nickname as the mother calls it across wheat fields. The nickname, as a gift from the mother, offers an escape from the proper name and its deadening role.

Shepard's "sense of heredity as both a blessing and a curse" (Oumano 7) pervades his work[11] and manifests itself in *Motel Chronicles* as the opposing desires for aloneness and for community. The motif of "separateness" punctuates several moments in the text that dwell on the inarticulateness and futility of expressing emotion. In the third-person, ten-page narrative about the trip to see his father in New Mexico, Shepard, "the driver," ponders "separateness" in his monologue:

> I thought of this girl. This Mormon girl. It wasn't particularly sexual.
> The thoughts were soft. I saw her pink lips. Her arms upstretched.
> I thought of trying to reach her although I knew she'd moved away
> a long time ago. I remembered her voice. I wondered if she ever
> thought of me. And I knew right then that things were very separate
> from each other. The most intimate things were very broken off [96].

Separateness sabotages the beckoning moment of intimacy with the girl, described in terms of a "soft" and "pink" flower. Only intermittently can remembrance overcome separateness. Only in memory does he have an intimate relationship with the girl who "moved away": "I remembered her voice." This overwhelming emotional isolation parallels the separate lives of Shepard's divorced parents, his futile attempts to establish a relationship with his father, and his general disillusionment with family. His conclusion that human beings cannot connect emotionally reaffirms the inevitability of separateness. His epiphany is the realization "right then" that things are inevitably separate and that "the most intimate things [are] very broken off."

He strives to balance his equally intense impulses toward community and aloneness. He detests the constraints of religion and the family and sees upbringing as a potentially strangling web: "[Religion] was another kind of prison to get out of.... [Y]ou have this personality, and somehow feel locked into it, jailed by all of your cultural influences and your psychological ones from your family ... I feel that isn't the whole of it, you know, that there's another possibility" ("Metaphors" 208).[12] That other possibility is an existence without separateness, like the one he yearns for when he thinks "soft" thoughts about the Mormon girl. The tension between Shepard's unrealizable dream of total connectedness and the doom of inevitable separateness reveals gaps at the center of his autobiographical web; the demands for autonomy conflict with the longing for connectedness and community.

Birth and Autonomy

Shepard parallels Stein in his obsessive wish to control and rewrite his engendering; two versions of his birth appear in *Motel Chronicles*.[13] One account depicts him as independent and already separate from his mother upon emergence from the womb. However, he captures effectively the universal desire to regain the tranquility and connectedness associated with the mother and another mother figure, his mother-in-law Scarlett, O-Lan Johnson's mother. In a short narrative about a "girl friend" (53) who presses Shepard for exact information about his birth to draw up his astrological chart, he combines the factual hospital version of his birth with his own fictionalized one. Shepard wants the details of his birth to remain vague, and tells her he was born "way out in the boondocks somewhere. Somewhere obscure" (52). He refutes as "fictitious" the information she obtains from the head nurse about the date and time of his birth, citing mysterious "verification from other sources (not my Mother)" (52). In this unofficial version of his birth, he alters the time of his birth from three in the afternoon to a bleak, cold, and desolate 2:47 a.m. during war curfew hours. Using the "anonymous sources" (52) or "mysterious witnesses to [his] birth" (53) as authorities, he rewrites his birth to give himself instant autonomy, mobility, judgment, and consciousness. Upon his emergence from his mother's body, his mother "fall[s] unconscious" (52), and without a nurse in attendance Shepard takes "full advantage of [his] new mobility in the outside" (52).

The phrase "in the outside" gives the mother's body the status of place and defines it by contrast as "inside." His ambivalence about the site of birth mirrors the human being's analogous relationships to the earth and to the female body; both are alien environments and homes.[14] Shepard's birth scene epitomizes what Leonard Lutwack calls, in a discussion of the human being's relationship with place, "an infant's experience of the mother's body as the first environment": "Harboring the child within her body, woman is herself a place, an enduring place, from the child's point of view" (82). Thus, Shepard's first moments of existence are migratory ones, a leaving of one place to explore an unknown and threatening one. In recounting this initial moment of life, he encapsulates the "universal

American experience": "looking forward to a new place and looking back at the old place" (Lutwack 144). Shepard portrays himself as trying in his first moments of consciousness to transcend the birth place/earth/mother; autonomy hinges on his ability to independently reach new territory. He drags himself across the room to the windows with the strength of a newborn's arms and initiates himself, through pain, into life: "I began to get my first taste of what it's like to suffer" (*MC* 53).

His account of his birth emphasizes his autonomy and choice to detach himself completely from the mother. The issue of separateness recurs: "I watched her body. I knew I'd come from her body but I wasn't sure how. I knew I was away from her body now. Separate" (53). In this account, separateness takes on a positive connotation; it constitutes a necessary yet traumatic step in identity formation rather than the state of emotional deprivation that is his father's legacy to him. The sound of warplanes outside the windows attracts the attention of the infant Shepard and catapults him into the "tremendous panic" of being between "two worlds" (53). He is torn between his mother, "the world [he'd] left behind," and the "new one" (53), the vista and territory outside the window associated with the world of the father.[15] Thus, Shepard remains suspended between the passive mother, identified as an empty womb, a static place, a safety he left "head first" and "covered with blood" (52), and the world outside the windows, a landscape of possibility, with the windows "directly overhead" opening onto the vista of a wartime world associated with his father. Only through severing himself from the mother and relegating her to the status of a body/place can he attain the manhood possible in the world outside the windows too high for him to reach.

Attributing an adult perspective to himself as a newborn emphasizes his power to will himself into being — in effect, to give birth to himself. Shepard's knowledge from "other sources" of his first minutes of life is limited because his witnesses "claim they lost track of my progress" (53). However, an adult perspective enfolds that of the infant Shepard: "I knew I wasn't a colt ... knew I wasn't a frog or a bird for sure" (52). The invention of an evolved infant consciousness reinforces his control, self-awareness, and autonomy.

Shepard projects the paternal-maternal conflict (also prevalent in his plays) onto the landscape, viewing it both as something to abandon and as desired destiny. Uncommitted to the mother's or the father's world, to connectedness or the devastating alternatives, he hangs suspended, his identity an amorphous potentiality. He rejects the mother as origin *and* the father as destiny and refuses to identify with the realm of emotional connectedness or with the predetermined symbolic order.

Shepard weaves these psychological strands throughout the text; in fact, his father and his pervasive memories of his mother are the dominant motifs of *Motel Chronicles*. His mother's constant presence asserts itself through Shepard's reveries, and because his memories of her date from his childhood, she never transcends the mother role to be portrayed as a separate person. She remains sealed in the past, a dependable source of untraumatic memories and emotional comfort. Although two photographs of his father appear in the text, he remains nevertheless an absence that Shepard attempts to fill through the narratives pertaining to him and the photographs of him.[16] Shepard's memories of his father disrupt the present and indicate the unresolved nature of the father-son relationship.

The fragmentary nature of the narratives about Sam Sr. and the photographs that attempt to capture the coherence of the father merely emphasize the emotional fragmentation inherited by the son from the father. The several narratives that mention Sam Sr. lack a vivid portrait either of the father himself or of the father-son relationship. Instead, they focus on the settings and props surrounding Sam Sr. In one narrative Shepard's father gives his son a "tour" (55) of the pictures on the walls of his desert residence, including the "collage of faces splattered with bacon grease" (55). The wall decorations range from nature scenes "ripped from a 1954 *Arizona Highways*" to "a flight of B-52 Bombers in Wing Formation" (55); each picture on the wall is a puzzle piece in the enigma of the father. Shepard's definitive statement about his dad highlights what he does not know more than what he does know about him: "My Dad lives alone on the desert. He says he doesn't fit with people" (56).[17] Shepard attempts to fill the emotional void of his father's identity with descriptions of a few of his father's mannerisms: "[H]e [runs] his hand across the bristles" (55) of his World War II fighter-pilot haircut. The gaps, ellipses, and mysteries of his father's identity are the only verifiable facts of his personality. The photograph accompanying the final lines of the "wall-tour" narrative silently intrudes into the intimate father-son encounter by reminding the reader of the witness who was there to take the photograph. This intrusion "stages" an image that embodies the desire propelling the book: father and son emotionally connected.

This photograph verifies Shepard's quest to find the elusive father who represents in his pitiful way the clichéd cowboy mentality that thrives on independence and isolation. Motifs defining the father as physically and emotionally isolated and inaccessible resurface throughout the book — his continued identification with his role as a fighter pilot and the romance of World War Two, his social isolation, and his drinking problem ("He spent all the food money I'd gave him on Bourbon" [55]). However, Shepard's portrait of his father never advances beyond a repetition or reshuffling of those motifs. The desired father remains disassembled and inaccessible. The photographs of Sam Sr. merely represent Shepard's futile dreams to know him. They mark the text with the search for, not the presence of, the father.

In the third-person narrative about a truck ride during which the family group "visit[s] the father of one of the men" (91), photographs again express an unrealized desire for the father and his consequent emotional absence, as well as the objectification of Shepard's own emotional longing. The travelers attempt to "take some pictures of the whole family together" (92). The family pictures represent the desire for the mythical and unified family, but the absence of family pictures in the text counterpoints the longing for connectedness on the part of the travelers: "They tried to get the old man out of the room into the sunshine so they could take some pictures of the whole family together. He stumbled just outside the door and fell into a curtain of aluminum flip-tops from empty beer cans that he'd strung together himself. He cursed the gravel under his feet and staggered toward a little patch of brown grass" (92). The solitary father's difficulty with and resistance to going out into the sunshine to be photographed with the family symbolizes the impossibility of the family ever achieving oneness, figuratively or literally.

The father ruptures and fragments *Motel Chronicles*, but mother figures open, close, frame and unify the text that is itself a gift to Shepard's mother, dedicated: "for my mother / Jane Elaine." He omits from the dedication both the dreaded legal name that we "die with" and her maiden/father's name, Schook. In the book's opening narrative, Shepard and his mother, a mother-infant dyad, travel together across the Badlands and stop "on the prairie at a place with huge white plaster dinosaurs standing around in a circle" (9). The piece, perhaps Shepard's first memory, combines imagination, actual memory, and facts gathered later to counteract the vagueness of the memory. Shepard includes (as he does in the birth scene) the perspective of the child who either remembers, or has gradually convinced himself that he remembers, things that he has been told: "I was teething then and the ice numbed my gums" (9). He makes assumptions about the attitude of his young mother in the narrative: "She hummed [a song] very softly to herself. Like her thoughts were far away" (9).

The scene captures the ideal union of mother and child before the traumatizing intervention of the father. (Shepard's father did leave for the war in Europe immediately after his son's birth.) Indeed, the symbiotic union of mother and child while they walk among the dinosaurs corresponds to Lacan's "imaginary" or Freud's pre–Oedipal stage.[18] Significantly, his first memories are not only of his mother, but of being "on the road" with her as they traveled from military base to military base. Thus, his early life sets a precedent for the displacement and mobility central to his adult identity and to the characters in his plays. He rides on "the shelf behind the back seat of the Plymouth" and stares up at the stars. His mother carries him in the cold night wrapped in a brown Army blanket and hums a tune he now thinks was "Peg o' My Heart." He and his mother, like a united being in the cold and desolate night, perform a surrealistic dance among the "huge white plaster dinosaurs": "We weaved slowly in and out through the dinosaurs. Through their legs. Under their bellies. Circling the Brontosaurus. Staring up at the teeth of Tyranosaurus [*sic*] Rex. They all had these little blue lights for eyes" (9). The bond between mother and son overrides what might have been a frightening scene for a young child. He recalls or invents only the blissful togetherness: "There were no people around. Just us and the dinosaurs" (9).

Shepard does not have to rely on photographs to "picture" his mother as he must to remember his father. During a motel stay, he intricately describes how he washes a shirt and presses it between towels with his feet to squeeze the water out of it:

> He washed his red shirt in the sink. Laid a motel towel on the floor. Laid the shirt on the towel. As he smoothed the sleeves and crossed them on the belly of the shirt he thought of his own death. Of how they might cross his arms just like the sleeves on his own dead belly. He laid a second towel on top of the red shirt so the shirt was sandwiched then walked on top of the towel with his bare feet, making tight mincing steps, squeezing the water out. This was something he'd picked up from his mother. He'd seen her do this with her own bare feet on top of blue fuzzy sweaters with small synthetic shells for buttons. He'd seen her toes curl. Watched water squish out faintly bluer than water. Bleeding from dye. He thought of her feet and *pictured* them so vividly that his whole mother appeared before him [22; emphasis added].

The ritual he learned from her brings her image before him and becomes a ritual of death or mourning as his and his mother's bodies conflate. Just as his clothes stand in for an alternate self, the remembered image of his mother's "blue fuzzy sweaters with small synthetic shells for buttons" stands in for her body. Through the metaphor of clothes and the ritual associated with those clothes, Shepard resurrects his mother: the "bleeding from dye" that oozes from the sweater recalls the mother's blood that drenched Shepard upon emergence from the womb in the fictionalized hospital birth scene. Fragment by fragment, he pieces together his mother, eventually conjuring her up in entirety, and even displaces her body with his own. His own "bare feet" mimic his mother's actions and transform into a vision of her bare feet in which "her toes curl." He creates her presence at will. Unlike the father, she is eternally accessible for his emotional dependence. But even in Shepard's evocations of her powerful presence, she remains without the autonomy granted the distant father.

However, male violence intrudes on this same motel scene of reverent communion and mergence with the mother. Suddenly "a form burst through the door. A man the size of a train. Two fists blasted him in the shoulders. Then one to the side of his head. He went down. He hit the air conditioner with his knee. His nose hit the edge of a glass table. He was kicked once in the back. The form spoke: 'You ever mess with Virgie agin, I'll kill ya!'" (24). The source of violence remains unnamed: "a man" or "a form" enters the room. "Two fists," not an entire person, strike him in the shoulders. The passive voice in "He was kicked in the back" displaces and depersonalizes the brutal action. Shepard denies and represses the violent male presence: he contains and diminishes the brutality in the account by disassociating the actions from human agency. In contrast, however, Shepard nurtures and maximizes each fragment of female presence to evoke a source of comfort.

A narrative about running away from school also delineates this emotional opposition of the mother and father and denies the masculine source of violence. He describes the violent welcome he received when the police had to call his parents to pick him up: "I got whipped three times with the buckle-end of my Dad's belt.... That was it. Then he left the house. He never said a word" (31). The father's silence and absence were evident early in Shepard's life. Even the pain the father inflicts Shepard attributes to an inanimate "buckle-end" rather than his enraged father. His mother, though she does not speak in the narrative (indeed, she is silent throughout the text), is ever present. "Listening" to her comforts Shepard as a child: "I lay in bed listening to my mother ironing in the kitchen. I *pictured* her ironing. The hiss of steam. The sprinkle bottle she used to wet my Dad's shirts. I *pictured* her face staring down at the shirt as her arm moved back and forth in a steady tempo" (31; emphasis added). Shepard has internalized the image of his mother so that image travels with him from motel room to motel room just as the two traveled together in Shepard's infancy; however, his father always eludes the present moment or place. Through his imagination, Shepard evokes his mother's presence (as when he presses water from the shirt); his father, even when present, remains emotionally unavailable or located in another era.[19] His mother pervades the everyday and concrete: even fragments of her — feet pressing water from the blue sweater, the sounds of her ironing — comfort Shepard like a lullaby. Yet his father, the stereotypic loner bomber pilot, is an impenetrable violent person Shepard can never grasp.

Motel Chronicles ends with a 17-page narrative and a short poem about Shepard's mother-in-law Scarlett Johnson, who suffered a cerebral hemorrhage in September 1979 that resulted in aphasia and loss of memory.[20] Without extratextual biographical information, the reader automatically assumes that this narrative is about Shepard's mother. Although writing in first-person, Shepard distances himself from the painful account. He camouflages the "I" in "we," refers to Scarlett as "she," avoids all proper names, and never states the exact relationship of any of the people involved.

Nevertheless, Shepard's vulnerability, sorrow, and frustration are diffused throughout his account of her illness and partial recovery. Scarlett, too, becomes one of the "lost" people still known to him in name and appearance (Daniels 129). But she is also a person who, over time, has mysteriously vanished because of her loss of memory, self, language, and sense of time. Observing the fragility of Scarlett Johnson's identity, Shepard poignantly recognizes the fragility of the family unit and the identities defined by it. He seems particularly horrified that he and his family could go out for a bike ride and return to find that Scarlett's familiar identity has been "shattered." His reactions to her ordeal and his subsequent role in her recovery (for example, by helping her to regain her power of speech) perhaps triggered the identity crisis he describes to Chaikin: "one's identity being shattered under severe personal circumstances" (Daniels 128). The experience threatens him with identity loss too, for after her hemorrhage, Scarlett, a constant presence in his life since his marriage to O-Lan Johnson in 1969, does not recognize him or anyone else in the family. The experience destabilizes Shepard's identity, for he loses the recognition and reassurance one gains through the eyes of others.[21]

In this closing narrative, Shepard reverses the mother-son dyad with which the book opens by becoming a nurturing father figure to his mother-in-law, a role that has obvious therapeutic effects for him. Scarlett devolves and replaces the present with the past by repeating it: "Every day she would ask us again about her mother. She would ask us if we knew for sure she was dead. She'd ask us where she was buried. How long ago. What city she died in. She couldn't believe it. For days she mourned for her mother who had died a long long time ago" (MT 141). Having lost the linear narrative and logic of her life, Scarlett returns, as Shepard and Stein can do only textually, to the site of emotional trauma: the loss of the mother. Remembering restores Scarlett's functional self.

Shepard opens his text with a memory of his mother so delicate, precious, and ephemeral that it must be nourished to completeness: the dream-like dance among the looming dinosaurs on the dark prairie, the embrace of his mother. He ends the text with a memory so painful that the narrative moves toward eradication of itself: "Then she'd [Scarlett] touch her scar. Run her fingers slowly down the barren skin and ask us how she got it. We told her but she didn't remember. We told her the names of the doctors. She didn't remember. We told her she was home now but she didn't remember. Her head would fold forward so that her chin rested on her breastbone. Tears flooded her knees. This posture told her whole story" (141). Scarlett tells her story without words, even without memory. Her life has led not to the culmination of a life's narrative, but to a barrenness, an absence of memory that gives her only pain. It is Shepard who remembers, who writes this narrative "exactly one year" later in order not to forget and who experiences emotional catharsis through his vicarious mourning with her. But it is Scarlett who wears the physical scar signifying that she "didn't remember." She embodies in a single person the pain and trauma represented by each of Shepard's parents: the severance from the union that is "mother" and the vacuum of identity that is "father."

His mother-in-law apparently serves as a replacement mother figure onto which Shepard projects his unresolved maternal-paternal split.[22] It is significant that Scarlett, unlike his mother, is not silenced (even though it is *she* who suffers aphasia) or confined to the role of Shepard's nurturer. In Scarlett, to whom *he* became nurturer, Shepard more completely confronts the pain inherent in losing the bliss he associates with his mother. And he deals more honestly with the reality of women's bodies; he perceives Scarlett as a complex being — body, mind, memory, pain — in contrast to the fetishized Mormon girl (a "pink flower") and his mother's body (fragmented and interpreted according to Shepard's sporadic emotional needs).

Shepard's ambivalence about a proper name, his violently contradictory feelings about the family, and his failure to establish a consistent identity relation in his autobiographical writings challenge the legitimacy of the paternal name, a name that for Shepard represents death. He recognizes and even laments the separateness of the mother's and father's worlds, representing, respectively, the ideal and the absent and inaccessible. In refusing the author's and his father's name, he refuses on a personal level his destiny and the death inscribed in the name; on a textual level, he refuses and endlessly defers a narrative destiny for his autobiography.

A quirky, impressionistic collage of autobiography, fantasy, photographs, poems, and fragments, *Motel Chronicles* defies genre classification. Its structure borders on randomness, and Shepard's relative disregard for his audience foregrounds his introverted method and personal motives for writing the book. Generally overlooked except as a supplementary text that elucidates Shepard's other work or his private life, the text has a genre label that conveniently fluctuates depending on the reader's point of view. The bibliography of King Kimball's *Sam Shepard: A Casebook* ambiguously describes it as "a collection of poetry and prose" (xxxiii). Don Shewey identifies it as "the journal [Shepard] kept when he started spending a lot of time in rented rooms while making movies" and pinpoints the nature of the genre dilemma when he states that an actual trip Shepard took with his wife, mother-, and father-in-law "*probably* formed the basis of a father-son encounter described in *Motel Chronicles* (*Sam Shepard* 162, 147; emphasis added). Ron Mottram sees this "collection of published prose" as a particularly useful source for "our understanding of both the man and his work" (2) and endows it with full autobiographical status: "a collection of autobiographical prose pieces and poems" (169). Gary Grant illuminates the composition of the text:

> For the published version of *Motel Chronicles* (1982) Shepard selected stories, poems and notes from a hardcover notebook written at home in Mill Valley, California and during various trips to Texas and New Mexico from August 1978 to May 1981. This material was published from the handwritten copy without corrections or editing, thereby maintaining in *Motel Chronicles* the spontaneous and improvisational tone of other unpublished notebooks in the Boston University Collection [551].

The free-form organization and multi-generic content suggest Shepard's skepticism about narratives (autobiographical and otherwise), and about the meanings we attempt to derive from them. His failure to adopt a familiar developmental pattern in the text — chronological or even geographical, as a travel narrative would have — resists formal generic status. Despite the word *chronicles* in the title, the text only hints at chronological order.[23] An account of Shepard's birth does not appear until many pages into the text, but the text does begin with the piece about traveling as a small child with his mother across the Badlands. Beginning the text with this scene from early childhood is the only sign of the chronological order expected of autobiographical works. The text follows no organizational principle. The pieces are not categorized according to time of composition, Shepard's age in the piece, facet of self (such as the adult actor, the child), point of view ("I," "we"), geographical location, or theme. To a reader unfamiliar with critical articles focusing on the inbreeding of Shepard's artistic material and private life, *Motel Chronicles* might easily pass as a loose collection of narrative pieces about various fictional characters.

Shepard unearths and explores his cast of past and present selves in a process that contradicts what Judith Kegan Gardiner calls the repressive dynamic characteristic of male memory: "[M]ale memory operates differently from female memory, at least in terms of the memory of emotional states.... Men maintain a coherent sense of themselves by repression" (358–59).[24] Shepard's theories on identity, as evident in the text and in his dramatic works, do not operate by repression; instead, he purposely multiplies the strands of his life. His perception of writing as "play" enhances the evocation of memory and emphasizes his deliberate departure from the phallogocentric narrative model: "The reason I began writing plays was the hope of extending the sensation of *play* (as in 'kid') on into adult life. If 'play' becomes 'labor,' why play?" ("Language" 214). Kerouac's "jazz-sketching with words," an approach that Shepard, a former rock musician, equates with musical jamming ("Language" 217), heavily influences his compositional and organizational style. His narrative structures "reflect the way Americans experience everyday life — in fits and spurts, and surface impressions" (Marranca, "Alphabetical" 23). In this sense, Shepard's pluralistic identity is a logical, contemporary psychological response to a fragmented reality.

Shepard resembles Hellman in merging factual memories with an idealized version of events, often to the point that he leaves in question the degree to which he invents the incidents he recounts. When writing about an idealized American village, for example, he describes "reveries" that echo Virginia Woolf's "moments of being": "Small moments open for me sometimes in crossing the kitchen when the sun hits a particular color in the paint job" (*MC* 68). The account of the village may be fantasy, fact, or a mixture of both: "I go into a reverie from pastel blue of a time of Dairy Cows, very few people, all who knew each other, in a small isolated American Village" (68). The place he dreams of seems stereotypically rural American, complete with "a horse named 'Nigger,'" "Old women I go on errands for," "A Parrot even older than the women," and "Sycamore leaves as broad as my chest" (68). Yet, the idiosyncratic and idyllic scene has the ring of a fairy tale: "A smell of women. All old. The smell of old women on everything" (68).

However, his detailed description of his "dead Aunt, sitting upright, a lamp lit on her shoulder, one hand limp in her lap" (68), introduces an autobiographical note and suggests that this narrative is a reminiscence about a visit to relatives when he was a small boy. He remembers how "confused" he felt that "even in death her knees seemed young," and recalls his feeling repulsed by "the small rolls of flesh that erupted out of the tops of her shoes," a consequence of wearing shoes too small for her feet — what he calls "Betty Boop Mythology" (68). He attributes his self-knowledge as an adult to this early experience: "It was this contradiction between her feet and her knees that led me to see broader contradictions in myself. Later, I secretly thanked her feet for this" (68). Thus, the perspectives of the small boy and the adult bind together. He evokes the comforting presence of women (as with his mother) in an idealized scenario in which the integration of child and adult perspectives generate self-understanding.

This fragmented text that rejects chronological, spatial, or thematic organization resembles instead a map in which narratives, poems, or photographs form infinite and unpredictable connections. Shepard counteracts the text's seeming randomness and anchors his various identities in space and time by meticulously dating each piece and noting the place of composition: "1/15/80 / Homestead Valley, Ca." (16) or "4/14/82 / Bluewater, New Mexico thru / 4/18/82 / Barstow, Ca." (96). These place-time signatures privilege the date and place of composition — the act of writing — over the narrative authority. But his attention to the specifics of composition camouflages his treatment of places more as stimuli for communion with various selves rather than as significant physical realities. Some sites or locales in the text are points of topophilia. The time-place signatures also contradict and compensate for the often evasive or unlocatable narrative authority in the work. Individual pieces of the text become components that trace not only physical movement, but the mental movement in the writing act — the revisiting of various selves.

Duplicating microcosmically the American expansion forced back upon itself, the narrative energy of *Motel Chronicles* doubles back on itself,[25] rather than following a linear development. The book's fragmented structure embeds cul-de-sacs in the text and forces the forward movement of the autobiographical narrative to deflect and circulate among the spatial, temporal, and emotional points each poem, narrative, or photograph represents. Thus, *Motel Chronicles* embodies the "aimless and often destructive" movement in modern literature that "arrives nowhere" (Lutwack 223). The reader scans the text as one would read a map, the focus moving among the nodes on the textual map. Like Stein who plots her map of memory on America's landscape, Shepard repeatedly returns to the issues of his own engendering and placement in the symbolic order — to his birth and his identity contained in the proper name. Those issues are sites of rupture, trauma, or erasure.

Shepard's comments on his composition process attest to his use of all writing as a kind of autobiography, with each small text functioning as a reference point on his internalized map of memory. The importance of "immediate environments" binds writing and place: "I remember the exact place and time of every play. Even the people I was with. It's almost as though the plays were a kind of *chronicle* I was keeping on myself" ("Language" 219; emphasis added). In 1985, looking back on his writing career, Shepard again stresses the link in memory between place and writing: "The strongest impressions I have now of these early plays are of the specific times and places where they were written" (*Unseen Hand*, Introduction ix). He experiences his plays as "a series of impulsive *chronicles* representing a chaotic, subjective world" (ix; emphasis added). In Shepard's case, the recurring word *chronicle* lends a double interpretation to his role as author of *Motel Chronicles* and joins the subjective and objective perspectives: the private role of chronicler of the self and the public role of contemporary historiographer.

Shepard repeatedly escapes the role of authoritative autobiographer even as he ostensibly creates it; he disperses his narrative authority into the text's cast of narrators, which include a first-person narrator identified with Shepard; an omniscient narrator, "he," whose experience may double for Shepard's and a fictional character's from a play or film; and an unidentified omniscient narrator, sometimes "we" or "he," who narrates the experience of a "former" Shepard.

The narrative that opens "I used to bring Nina Simone ice" recounts Shepard's loss of his busboy's job at the Village Gate because, mesmerized by Simone's singing, he knocked over a candle and spilled hot wax "all over a businessman's suit" (*MC* 79). Nina Simone's verifiable identity and Shepard's biography clearly connect this incident with Shepard's early days in New York City, where he moved in 1963, thus uniting the identity of author, the narrating "I," and the character in the narrative. Shepard's geographical and personal displacement coincide at this early point in his life. Also evident at this point is his lifelong fascination with the concept of shifting identities as opposed to a core self. He has left his family, moved from the West to the East Coast, and changed his name. Ironically, "the one song" that Simone sang that really "killed" him was, "You'd Be So Nice to Come Home To," a song that "froze" Shepard in his "tracks" (79).

More complex is the voice in the third-person narrative about a day of rehearsal for the film *Resurrection*. "He" doubles for both Shepard and a fictional character. Only extratextual sources documenting his work on the film reveal the narrative as autobiographical. Shepard juggles the thoughts and motives of "he," the actor (Shepard himself), and the character the actor plays. The actor ponders the transformation he feels obliged to undergo to assume a temporary identity: "He wondered if he was supposed to be playing himself. If that's what they hired him for" (11). He envisions his costume as the instrument by which he assumes an alternative identity, a "deflated version of himself" (11). Unsure about which identity to assume, his concept of fluid identity makes it difficult for him to act out convincingly the Character's motivation to kill someone: "What he needed to know was why did his Character want to kill her Character in the first place? Something about Christ I guess. That was in the script someplace. Something about her being Christ.... Why would he think she was Christ? He wasn't stupid. The Character wasn't stupid" (13). Through the magic of art, the motivations and thought patterns of actor, author, and character inevitably intertwine at the end of the narrative: "Suddenly he appeared to himself.... There was no more doubt who the Character was" (13). In creating this character, Shepard fulfills his idea of a character "that not only functions in this world but that is really 'himself'" (Daniels 123), who is both a fictional construct and an authentic self. He merges the self that art creates and the self that creates art. Who is the "he" who appears to himself? Which "he," actor (Shepard) or character, experiences the sudden realization of identity?[26]

The third narrative position appears in the book's final and longest narrative, and is significant because Shepard intertwines a plural and singular voice and focuses uncharacteristically on the emotions of the family unit. The narrative recounts Scarlett Johnson's aneurysm, subsequent surgery, and lengthy recovery. The story begins, "Exactly a year ago to this day the three of us left her alone in the house and rode our bicycles down to the marsh by the freeway" (126). Biographical material narrows the "her" to Scarlett, Shepard's mother-in-law, and the "we" to Shepard, O-Lan Johnson, and either their son Jesse Mojo or Scarlett's husband, Johnny Dark.

Together, these three narrative positions — the clearly autobiographical "I," the ambiguous "he," and the collective "we" — camouflage, juggle, and destabilize the narrative authority the reader attaches to the unlocatable or unverifiable proper name. Using such narrative tactics, Shepard disowns his role as a cohesive source and organizer of the text and effectively disappears. The evasive author becomes, in Michel Foucault's terms, "a nucleus of expression" (151–53), a "projection"[27] onto the text, or a "functional principle" (159), rather than a personalized identity. Bonnie Marranca has noted the difficulty of finding Shepard the author in this work: "Behind the emotional gesture is the radical ideal of the authorless work and the denial of the Author as Myth" ("Alphabetical" 13). Shepard himself observes that after periods of "jazz-sketching with words," he gets "the haunting sense that something in me writes but it's not necessarily me. At least it's not the 'me' that takes credit for it" ("Language" 217).

Photographs: Image and Absence, Exposure and Concealment

The photographs in *Motel Chronicles*, several of Shepard himself, further splinter and erode the narrative authority. The uncaptioned photographs do not become artifacts; one cannot be sure of their truth value. Are they authentic photographs from a family album, or are they staged just for this text? Or are they movie stills, and thus borrowed from a larger text? J. Gerald Kennedy points out the paradox of the photographic image: "In representing life ... and occasionally reflecting back the soul's own image — it simultaneously confirms the inevitability of time and death.... The photographic print is at once an undeniable proof of existence ... and an emblem of mortality" ("Roland Barthes" 392). The click of the camera is an instant of death in which a subject becomes an object (392). Every photograph, as Roland Barthes contends in *Camera Lucida*, embodies "the return of the dead" (9). For Barthes, "the Photograph (the one I *intend*) represents that very subtle moment when, to tell the truth, I am neither subject nor object but a subject who feels he is becoming an object: I then experience a micro-version of death (of parenthesis): I am truly becoming a specter" (14). Photographs at once defy and prolong life, engage with the reality of death and evade it by giving life to the image. They can reaffirm existence through self-representation or threaten existence — as when Stein sees her newsreel image — by reminding us of the false association between image and what we subjectively perceive to be the self. The photographs in *Motel Chronicles* visually document a transference that occurs on a narrative level: Shepard's migrating narrative authority establishes itself, slips away, and disappears altogether in a kind of death. Shepard speculates that this invisibility or evasiveness is germane to the writing act itself: "I think most writers, in a sense, have the desire to disappear ... to be absolutely anonymous, to be removed in some way: that comes out of the need to be a writer" (Brantley H26).

The book's cover foreshadows puzzling and inconsistent identity relations between the images and the names or pronouns in the text. The cover photograph sets the precedent for the text-photo pattern that extends throughout the text: a narrative, poem, or fragment accompanied by a related photograph.[28] Ron Mottram comments on how the cover of *Motel*

Chronicles exemplifies the problematic nature of finding Shepard in the text. Is Shepard simply playing a role?

> On the cover of *Motel Chronicles* is a photograph of Sam Shepard. He is seen in full length, looking at the camera; his right hand grasps a bottle of Coke, and his left is tucked casually in his pocket. Parked next to him is an old funeral coach with a Texas license plate, and in the background, as if part of another world, the dry, empty street of a small Texas town, washed out by the intense midday sun. Shepard's clothes are well-worn and baggy, perhaps even lived and traveled in for some time. Or are the clothes part of a costume and was the photograph taken during a break in the making of a film? Is Shepard on the road or in character [158]?

That the photograph appears "vintage" complicates matters. Is it aged deliberately to confuse the reader or simply to authenticate the scene? The image replaces, usurps, and supersedes the power of the proper name. Even before the reader opens the text, the photograph of Shepard's image multiplies the author into a complex and disunified self. Timothy Dow Adams points out the unique power that photographs share with autobiography: "In short, autobiography and photography are commonly read as though operating in some stronger ontological world than their counterparts, fiction and painting, despite both logic and a history of scholarly attempts that seem to have proven otherwise" ("Introduction" 467). This power can create the illusion of autobiographical truth, provoke the reader to "write" autobiography by making connections between photographs or between photographs and text, as happens in Shepard's text.[29]

Like the evasive, fluctuating pronouns of the narrators, the photographs allow Shepard to assume either the subjective or the objective position in the text, or even both positions simultaneously.[30] Even as the photographic images provide visible proof that a composing self exists outside the text, they call attention to the unbreachable gap between the Shepard who writes and the Shepard constructed in the text, a gap that Roland Barthes desires to bridge by escaping time and change in the stability of photographic images. Shepard seems to want from photographs the same stability that Barthes describes:

> What I want, in short, is that my (mobile) image, buffeted among a thousand shifting photographs, altering with situation and age, should always coincide with my (profound) "self"; but it is the contrary that must be said: "myself" never coincides with my image [*Camera Lucida* 12].

On the book's title page, Shepard formally acknowledges the photographer's authority as separate from his own: "With photographs by Johnny Dark." (Johnny Dark, of course, was then Shepard's father-in-law and stepfather to O-Lan Johnson.) The introduction of an additional authoritative, invisible presence into the text — a controlling agent behind the camera — further fractures the authorial voice. Because Dark is the equivalent of a ghostwriter, it is never clear just how far his authority extends in the making of the text.

The photographs also determine to some extent the autobiographical or fictional status of *Motel Chronicles*. The poem about "my natural woman" seems at first to be a general complaint about a type of woman Shepard associates with Los Angeles:

> I've about seen
> all the nose jobs
> capped teeth
> and silly-cone tits
> I can handle
> I'm heading back
> to my natural woman [102].

Aware of Shepard's well-known disgust with the lifestyle he associates with L.A. and the movie industry, the reader might interpret the poem as a tirade against a stereotypical "L.A. Woman," or as an argument for a more "natural" lifestyle. However, the photograph of a "natural woman" opposite the poem forces an identification between the poem and the specific image of woman in the photograph, that is, between image and biographical fact. The young woman with long hair who wears jeans, boots, and a leather jacket drapes herself, like a domestic centerfold, across a washer, dryer, and ironing board. To a reader familiar with Shepard's biography, she instantly suggests O-Lan Johnson, who had been Shepard's wife since 1969. (At the time Shepard wrote the poem, "11/23/81," he was still living with Johnson.) In the absence of authoritative captions for the photographs, the mere juxtaposition of a photograph and narrative prompts the reader to connect names in the text with people in the photographs. The forced connection between image and biography usurps the narrative and actually manufactures autobiography, making irrelevant the issue of whether the woman in the photo is in fact Johnson.

One puzzling example of a photograph's ability to obscure rather than clarify the autobiographical aspects of the work is the one following the third-person, ten-page narrative about two men and two women on a road trip of several days. On the trip they "visit the father of one of the men"

(91), obviously Shepard's father.[31] Is the man in dark glasses sitting on the front bumper of a large truck Johnny Dark, one of two men in the narrative? (And if it is Dark, who actually took the photograph?) Certain aspects of the three-page monologue at the end of the narrative identify the second man, "the driver," as Shepard. Making typical Shepard movie references, the driver compares a man's facial expression to that of "Walter Houston's face in *Treasure of Sierra Madre*" (95). He mentions his sensuous thoughts about "this Mormon girl" (96), a reference to the "Tuesday Weld-type-of-blonde girl" in a preceding narrative about a train trip Shepard took from the West to the Midwest (43). And, he exhibits Shepard's obsession with cars in a tribute to the '58 Impala that borders on fetishization: "That was the first hot year for the Impala. 350 engine I think. Which was big for those days. Had that really beautiful rear end with the chrome curling down around those three red tail lights on each side" (93). The camaraderie that "Shepard" and "Dark" enjoy while driving all night while "the women" sleep hints at ways in which Dark may provide (as does his wife Scarlett) a healthier and more accessible parental image than Shepard's father does (96).

The numerous cross-references among the pieces in *Motel Chronicles* weave an autobiographical network by exploiting the very narrative fragmentation that undermines the construction of a unified autobiographical self. A casual out-of-doors family photograph accompanies the narrative with the most numerous and direct references to Shepard's family and is the only piece in which Shepard explicitly mentions family other than his mother and father: "my sister-in-law," "my wife," "my parents," and "the one son of mine" (124). The image of "my natural woman" a few pages earlier fills the vacuum of identity introduced by this single mention of "my wife." Is the woman standing in the back row with Shepard a more mature version of "natural woman" O-Lan Johnson? Biographical data, image, and narrative — the inter- and extra-textual — converge. The convergences fill gaps through cross-references, but leave many questions unanswered. Shepard both exerts authoritative presence as "I" in the written parts of the text and effects absence, existing as the object of another author's text (Dark's photograph).

Shepard's ambiguous, uncommitted narrative position in this family narrative is mirrored in his ambivalence about family identity: "These days I wonder about leaving. But I've seen myself when I leave. Already seen myself" (124). The writing subject experiences simultaneous presence and absence; he envisions presence through the writing act and the frozen image of the photography, and absence in his imagination. He contemplates his ambivalence about family unity amid the sounds of a buzzing and peaceful household: "My parents live apart. Separate lives. In a flash I almost feel I have a grip. The kind of grip that turns on its tail" (124). He fails to find identity, whether through the community of the family as represented by a photograph of the family group or within his individual self. Even family lacks the cohesiveness necessary to counteract alienation. His opposing impulses, to nestle into and to flee the family, remind us that family photographs possess a "patent familiarity" but are also "provocatively unfamiliar" (511). Thus, "they enforce the gap between ourselves in the present and those figures of the past, the gap between ourselves now as we look and ourselves as we were formerly looked at" (S. Smith, "Re-Citing" 511). The "separate"-ness of things, his impulse to leave, and his desire to duplicate the separateness inherited from his family haunt him. As "identity fragments" or "disidentity fragments," the photographs are the perfect visual equivalent of Shepard's sense of being a galaxy of selves (511).

However, it is the two photographs of the father and son that represent, along with the longing for the mother's presence, the dominant motifs of *Motel Chronicles*: the search for the father and the return to origins. Both narratives about "My Dad" (55–56, 118) are followed by photographs obviously made at the same location and probably on the same day, since Shepard and his father wear their same clothes in each of the photographs. The narratives are written more than one year apart in different states, and they are separated by 62 pages in the text; yet, the photographs that accompany them unite them into one text. This framing achieves what Siegfried Kracauer calls "endlessness," an ability to overcome the fragmentation inherent in photography, and it refers to the world outside the frame (264)—in this case a nonexistent closeness between father and son. The obvious similarity between the photographs converts the two narratives into the substantial textual presence of Shepard's eccentric, anti-social father. The associative logic of memory overcomes the spatial, chronological, and textual fragmentation of *Motel Chronicles* and creates a portrait of father and son.[32]

The crisscrossing narrative energy among the separate pieces in *Motel Chronicles* resists all effort to naturalize the text. Shepard simultaneously defines all writing as autobiographical, undermines the autobiographical project, and yet refuses the unified narrative voice expected in autobiography. Curiously, the time-place signatures counterbalance the playful, random organization of the text and supply it with its only authoritative note. The text evokes what Barthes deems "a new space-time category peculiar to photography: spatial immediacy and temporal anteriority, the photograph being an illogical conjunction between the *here-now* and the *there-then*" ("Rhetoric" 278). The photograph creates a reality of "*having-been-there*" (278), whether the familial closeness is a lie or truth. Fluctuating pronouns and the play between writing and photographs encapsulate Shepard's psychological and physical positions: the here and the there, the committed and the uncommitted, the singular and the collective selves. Each of these positions contributes to the expanding "galaxy" of identities proliferated by the text.

Identity: The Self as a Fictional Character

Shepard's preliminary "Note to the Actors" in *Angel City* offers an alternative to the concept of "a 'whole character' with logical motives behind his behavior which the actor submerges himself into": the actor "should consider instead a fractured whole with bits and pieces of character flying off the central theme ... more in terms of collage construction or jazz improvisation" (*FFL* 61–62). Such is the way he portrays himself in *Motel Chronicles*—fragmented and improvised. As he explains to Joseph Chaikin, he seeks a multi-purpose "suitable 'character,' one that not only functions in this world but that is really 'himself'" (Daniels 123). This "suitable character" would abolish divisions between public and private selves. Shepard argues that multiple and overlapping identities are the norm, and he does not impose a fictional unity on the selves in his text.

Only the announcement of Sam Shepard's proper name on the cover and title page of *Motel Chronicles* definitively establishes his authority as the author-organizer of a text that resists any constant identity relation. As a "constant relation between the one and the many," the proper name "federates our complexity of the moment and our changes in time" (Lejeune 30), and fictionalizes a unified notion of self. Only the reader's belief in the myth of the constant relationship between the writing and written "I"s in an autobiographical text — in the case of *Motel Chronicles*, "I" and "he" and "we" — makes it possible to label a text autobiography. This imagined fictional continuity between the distinct personas (writer and subject) gives the illusion of what Georges Gusdorf calls "unity and identity across time" (35), a traditional assumption of autobiography.

Motel Chronicles celebrates known and unknown, remembered and unremembered identities. Remarking on his childhood habit of sleepwalking, Shepard points to his desire, even as a child, to contact and experience the full range of hidden or suppressed selves: "I couldn't stand the fact that I was missing out on these unconscious encounters" (17). He wants the "thrill of having a relationship with [his parents] outside the

ordinary. A different kind of encounter" (19)—in other words, the paradoxical experience of being his unremembered and mysterious sleeping
self, as well as his conscious one. Unrepressed thought, memory, fantasy,
and fact can be the avenue to alternative selves: "I'm surprised at my own
nostalgia for times I barely remember living. I never think of myself as
going through the Forties. The Forties are reserved for my parents' generation and pilots with fur-collared leather jackets, smiling in front of
prop planes" (68). A mixture of movie stereotypes, his father's actual experiences, and his own fantasies make up Shepard's vision of the Forties.

For Shepard, identity in life or in his dramatic works consists of a
series of roles that may be modified or replaced. For him, identity is simply "the story each of us tells about ourselves" (Wilson 146), not an inflexible institution where the self resides. For example, one of his identities,
the adolescent Shepard, appears in a "story" in which he and Tim Ford
steal an Austin Healey, obtain false I.D.s, and spend the day in Tijuana
(36–37). This identity resurfaces only once in the text, in the narrative
about running away from home with a school friend. Repeatedly in his
plays, Shepard points out not only the danger, but the advantage and flexi-
bility, of believing you are your image—in effect, not feeling the unbear-
able schism between the authentic self and a role.[33]

Unraveling the consistent relations assumed to operate in an autobiographical text, Shepard challenges the assumption of theorists of male
identity that "stability and constancy are desirable goals for human personality" (Gardiner 352). Like Stein, Shepard questions and rewrites his
origins; however, his theory of the self demands the fluid interchange of
those identities and roles instead of the eradication of one or the absorp-
tion of one by the other. (Critics who base their arguments on the opposition of male and female often deem this fluidity a female identity trait.)
Unlike Stein's absolute repudiation or repression of the maternal, paternal, and familial, Shepard's early rejection of and alienation from the patriarchal family involves a regretful acknowledgment of the anger and frustration arising from the inextricable bonds between an oppressive family
and culture. The swirl of personal memories released in *Motel Chronicles*
suggests that for Shepard the repression so crucial to male identity formation is not only futile, but undesirable. He perceives as salvation the
multiplicity of identity that Stein perceives as a threat to integrity.

People in *Motel Chronicles* have the changeable natures of Shepard's
dramatic characters, who often switch personalities, speech patterns, and
motivations in mid-air. Just as Hoss and Crow in *The Tooth of Crime* (in
Seven Plays) adopt or abandon jargons and identities, in *Motel Chronicles*
Shepard lives in the skins of all his selves at once—the teenager who steals

cars, the young father and husband who longs to go on the open road, the man remembering and searching for his father, the frustrated writer, and the actor disillusioned with the movie industry. Commenting on *True West*, he acknowledges and exploits the plurality of the self: "I wanted to write a play about double nature…. I just wanted to give a taste of what it feels like to be two-sided. It's a real thing, double nature. I think we're split in a much more devastating way than psychology can ever reveal. It's not so cute. Not some little thing we can get over. It's something we've got to live with" (Shewey, *Sam Shepard* 141). Personality is "false," "added on," and "contrived," Shepard told interviewer Michiko Kakutani; the struggle between falseness and truth in the human being "sets up a great contradiction in everybody between what they represent and what they know to be themselves" ("Myths" 26).

In the narrative about a day of rehearsal for the movie *Resurrection*, Shepard's objectification of himself reflects the split between Shepard the actor and the character he plays and hints at the creative subtext of a potentially unsettling situation: "His costume was waiting. It looked just like the clothes he had on, like a deflated version of himself. He switched the clothes he had on for the costume and felt just the same. Exactly the same. Maybe a little bit stiffer. Cleaner maybe too. He wondered if he was supposed to be playing himself. If that's what they hired him for" (*MC* 11). Shepard matter-of-factly acknowledges the ambiguous boundary between the role and the self, between fiction and reality. Unthreatened by self-representations, he implies that it is only for the sake of keeping order in our lives that we invent, with costumes and scripts, demarcations between roles. "He" focuses on the potentially creative and functional advantages of manipulating the relationship between real and fictional selves, thus suggesting that the artist's role is just this chameleon-like ability to experience the disintegration and violation of self. The clothes are "a deflated version of himself," an unrealized extension of himself, rather than an alien identity he must assume. Shepard's theory of fluid identity allows for the possibility that "he" might simultaneously occupy all identities.

His visit to two old friends in New York City, first Bill and then a former girlfriend, Joyce Aaron (unnamed in the text), epitomizes his concern for "the identification of *others* over time" and for the maintaining of a connection with people who are "lost" to him (Daniels 128). The two friends evoke memories in Shepard and maintain habits that identify them as the same friends; the places, names, and faces are stable factors, but the people he encounters are not the same people he once knew. Like snakes who have shed skins many times since his knowing them, his friends are people he knew "*then* but now [has] no idea who they might be" (Daniels

129). Clearly, they are "lost" to Shepard — dead in a sense — though they still live (129).

Ellen Oumano sees this account of visiting Joyce Aaron as an illuminating example of "how [Shepard] took the raw material of his life ... and reshaped it into a literary experience" (46). He combines two memories involving Joyce Aaron and melds them into one[34] — the day they split up and the day she takes hallucinogens and becomes temporarily catatonic. Like Hellman in reinventing "the hours of the deer," he privileges subjective "truth." Thus, he creates a hybridized fiction resulting from the combination of two separate factual memories. Did Shepard realize, as Aaron argues, that he "wove [the two separate incidents] together" (Oumano 46)? As with Hellman, much more important than adherence to verifiable facts is his privileging of truth *as he remembered it.* Shepard's theories about identity in dramatic roles and of fictional characters provide essential clues for understanding his problematic construction of identity in *Motel Chronicles.*

A companion piece to *Motel Chronicles, The Rolling Thunder Logbook* maps identity onto the American landscape. Shepard comments on America's "Bicentennial madness," a celebration of fabricated and commercialized history in which we try "to reassure ourselves that we sprang from somewhere" (*RTL* 45). In his account of this rock and roll tour, Shepard labels the Rolling Thunder Revue tour a "pilgrimage" and describes it in terms of mapmaking:

> Rolling Thunder is searching for something too. Trying to make connections. To find some kind of landmarks along the way. It's not just another concert tour but more like a pilgrimage. We're looking for ourselves in everything. Everywhere we stop. Even when we're moving. Trying to locate ourselves on the map. In time and space [45].

Geographical terminology and introspective language conflate; the geographical becomes the personal. As if writing autobiographies in the medium of movement, the artists look for themselves "in everything," projecting the internal concept of the self onto the ever-changing landscape of the road. They re-locate those selves by "making connections" between the self and the landscape, between "landmarks along the way" and themselves. The concert tour, literally a movement across geographical territory, becomes an inner journey. The artists seek private "connections," their own new versions of the "old road," not just connecting routes between locations on a map. Even the time and space, history and geographical orientation take on spiritual connotations. Like Shepard in *Motel*

Chronicles, the pilgrims in the Rolling Thunder Revue are dispersed selves who experience and collect fragments of the self at each "stop" and even in the spaces between stops. Viewed as a map, *Motel Chronicles*, too, is a collection of geographical stops which provides spiritual re-orientation and re-placement, an avenue to self-knowledge.

Joan Didion's
"Places of the Mind"

In their three unorthodox autobiographical works, Stein, Hellman, and Shepard each construct a self while envisioning America as a psychological map, a myth, an ideology, or a fiction. Additionally, these authors clarify and comment on the American experience and the conflation of physical and psychological geographies.

Each author's autobiographical strategies introduce new possibilities for imagining the connection between self and nation and how each defines the other. In a larger sense, the authors enact individually the ongoing identity crisis of America itself, suggesting that perhaps America and Americanism are themselves nothing more than the restless struggle with identity. Stein creates herself as the generic "good American" and American literary genius; Hellman founds her exemplary Americanism on the right to political dissent and posits a private, ever-revising identity; and Shepard, the post–World War II American male, is a multitude of private, fragmentary identities that constitute a "galaxy" of selves. Their American identities stem from dissent, displacement, and the disruption of the teleological momentum that makes possible the fiction of consistent, unified identity.

America's identity is grounded less in its geographical actuality than in its rejection of place, and thus was from its beginnings primarily an idea. But even as the Declaration of Independence announced the legal origin of the United States, it also announced that nation's derivation from another nation. Before it was endowed with a legal identity, America was

117

defined in terms of its own genealogy — somewhere that is "not Europe." Like Stein's, Hellman's, and Shepard's Americas, the collective America of the European transplants was rewritten as they constructed its identity. So, is America a unifying document or an act of rebellion, as defined by history? Is it Stein's map of memory? Hellman's ideology? Shepard's landscape mirroring a masculine/feminine dichotomy? It is all of these and more.

The inner landscapes of Stein, Hellman, and Shepard publicly register private anxieties; *Everybody's Autobiography, Scoundrel Time, and Motel Chronicles* fuse geography and psychology. Stein's map of memory traces her aversions as well as her passions. Traumatic memories transform into erasures; Oakland is no longer "there" and Cambridge is "lost" along with the young Stein who once lived there. As the representative American, she absorbs the particularity of cities, people, and regional American landscapes. For Stein, the connections between America's geography and the American character accounts, without reliance on social, hereditary, or historical influences, for the nature and behavior of the generic American, and by extension, of Stein herself. Hellman ameliorates loss and pain by weaving fact and fiction into a tangle that she admits can never be unraveled, even by herself. The "hours of the deer," the emotional center of her political memoir, politicizes the personal and forecasts the evolution of her autobiographical project into the deliberate invalidation of memory. Truth, she suggests near the end of her tumultuous life, cannot be found in remembered fact. The fulcrum of Shepard's text, the fictionalized hospital birth scene, projects the fundamental split he feels between the maternal and paternal, the collective and individual, fusion and individuation. He persists in his search for the "stillness" and peace belonging to a mythic and spiritual dimension of America. But he remains suspended in his emotional alienation, torn between his perceived opposition of feminine and masculine. He is unable to reconcile completely his conflicting impulses: a longing for placement and home, as associated with the feminine, and his need for the mobility, which is for him the realm of the displaced and absent father.

In Stein's and Shepard's cases, the careful, anxiety-ridden return to their births, as well as their meditations on the politics of naming — Stein's grandmother's *G* and Shepard's childhood nickname and adult name change — signal their fixations on controlling and altering the basis of everyday identity — birth and legal identity. In verifiable ways, they reinvent themselves. Hellman lessens anxiety by transforming *Scoundrel Time* into a palimpsestic text in 1979, adding a layer of commentary and revision; she thus sets a precedent for systematically maintaining control over the self she presents in her memoirs. Each author thus reduces an overwhelming complexity to a reassuring textualized unity.

Joan Didion's America: A Hologram on Air?

Joan Didion's contemporary vision of twentieth-century America offers a definitive example or culminating metaphor for the Americas of Stein, Hellman, and Shepard, for she reminds us that contemporary America exists, increasingly, less as a geographical reality than as an abstraction, a dream, or a malleable concept. Didion's autobiographical work defines the concern of the twentieth-century autobiographer and critic: to establish an equilibrium that preserves the integrity of "I" while necessarily incorporating the context of the "not-I"—history, family, nation, and culture. She maps a new intersection between genre, self, and place in her work: the nexus of the disassembling genre, the poststructuralist concept of self, and a consciousness of the roles geography and mapping play in writing the self and nation. Didion's paradigms are the reality that belies the enticing fictions of traditional autobiography.

In her more autobiographical essays spanning 1961–1992, many of which are collected in *Slouching Towards Bethlehem*, *The White Album*, and *After Henry*, Didion envisions America as a cultural abstraction, a reality that transcends physical geography and renders physical place irrelevant. The intersection of Didion's work with the concept of geographics raises important theoretical questions vital to both cultural studies and autobiography studies. Her vision of America as a hologram frames the autobiographical writings of Stein, Hellman, and Shepard, for they too write of an America and Americanism no longer predicated on stable geographical or cultural terms.

Even the organization of Didion's books emphasizes that actual places are best conceived of as "places of the mind" (*STB*) and transforms the incomprehensibility of vast physical and cultural geography into a comprehensible image. Headings such as "Seven Places of the Mind" and "California Republic" in the tables of contents of all three essay collections organize autobiography, history, political commentary, and journalism in terms of imaginary place, a mental geography, and link the personal and the geographical.

In interviews, she has revealed her habit of putting maps on the wall, a practice that reflects the geographical metaphors underpinning her work; she "writes about frontiers, whether they be cultural, psychological, political, or geographical" (Friedman, Ellen G., *Essays*, "Introduction" 1). During the early years of her career in New York City, she lived with a map of her native Sacramento County on the wall to, as she puts it, "remind me who I was" ("Goodbye to All That," *STB* 230). While writing *A Book of Common Prayer*, she worked with a map of "Central" America by her desk, a catalyst for transforming mapped geography into the imaginary Boca Grande she invents for the setting of her novel (Davidson 13). These habits emphasize the connection between geography and identity for Didion, and expose the "fetishism of mimesis" underlying our assumptions about maps — and autobiographies (Barnes and Duncan xii): that they are accurate mirrors of an objective reality rather than ideological, cultural, and political texts themselves.

In her essay "On the Road," an account of her national book tour in the 1970s which was characterized by endless radio interviews and travel, she pays homage to the unsettling of America. She conceives of an image signifying the ultimate transformation of physical place into a collective, impersonal entity: "'Out I-10 to the Antenna' was the kind of direction we had come to understand, for we were on the road, on the grid, on the air and also in it" (*WA* 179). In a vision oddly reminiscent of Stein's aerial view of the "Cubist" American landscape in the 1930s, physical place evaporates into a network of airports for Didion — into an image both comprehensible and modeled on other texts: "I began to see America as my own, a child's map over which my child and I could skim and light at will. We spoke not of cities but of airports" (*WA* 176). She envisions America as an enormous circuitry, the airports as the interchangeable nodes, points which function not as places in themselves but as transition points that make possible the escape from place.

Her version of "the road" reverses the quintessentially American concepts of frontier expansion and undermines the romance of the open road epitomized by the car culture, Kerouac and the Beat Generation — a romance Shepard has clearly internalized and responds to in *Motel Chronicles*. The impulse to cross and recross the continent renders irrelevant the geographical boundaries that make America conceivable in geographical terms: "I began to see the country itself as a projection on air, a kind of hologram, an invisible grid of image and opinion and electronic impulse" (*WA* 178). The hologram, a projection giving the illusion of three-dimensional integrity, is an appropriate metaphor for a nation. On the "invisible grid" the individual constructs a personal vision of America but also contributes to and is a part of the collectively written and remembered text/map that is America.

In Didion's America, the mall is "the frontier ... reinvented," and in the subdivisions surrounding it, twentieth-century American settlers can "recast their lives *tabula rasa*" ("On the Mall," *WA* 181). The shopping malls dotting America's landscape are less important as physical places than as artificial havens where one experiences a "sedation" of the pervasive American anxiety (*WA* 186). They are extensions of "the road" which, as Edward Relph has pointed out, is no longer the means to reach a place but is itself a place (*Place* 90). Indeed, the freeways mapping the modern pioneer sprawl and connecting the malls and suburbs of Los Angeles provide the only "secular communion" available to its residents: the freeway experience "requires a total surrender, a concentration so intense as to seem a kind of narcosis" ("Bureaucrats," *WA* 83). In this "exhilaration," this "rapture-of-the-freeway," as Didion calls it, "the mind goes clean, the rhythm takes over," and there is "a distortion of time" (*WA* 83). The common spiritual experience of Los Angeles derives from the intensity of the survival instinct necessary to stay alive and mobile: This "special way of being alive … the extreme concentration required in Los Angeles seems to bring on a state of heightened awareness that some locals find mystical" (Banham quoted in *WA* 83).

Whether speaking of Los Angeles, Miami, Washington, D.C., New York City, Hawaii, the California of her childhood, or enormous post–World War II suburban developments like Lakewood, California, Didion repeatedly insists that rather than a concrete place, late twentieth-century America is instead a collective delusion, a private dream, or a momentary intersection of common belief. The "true California" ("Notes from a Native Daughter," *STB* 180), as Didion calls it, the California she and generations of her family have known intimately, a California defined in terms of land, crops, lush valleys and the cycles of drought and rain, is profoundly real for her. Her habit of returning to her childhood home to finish her books, entering the cave of the room she slept in as a child, reveals her eccentric and touching effort to re-experience that California (Davidson 16; Kakutani, "Joan Didion" 34). But she has an enigmatic comment about people "back East" who think they have been to the golden California known by her family since the mid-nineteenth century: "They have not been [there], and they probably never will be" (*STB* 173).

Didion's doubts about the reliability of memory and its link to reality echo Hellman's acceptance, late in life, of how little literal fact has to do with one's subjective truth: "It is hard to *find* California now, unsettling to wonder how much of it was merely imagined or improvised, melancholy to realize how much of anyone's memory is no true memory at all but only the traces of someone else's memory, stories handed down on the family network" (*STB* 178). Here, Didion ponders the unsettling, and, for some autobiographers, terrifying, fiction that our memories are not our own but are inherited reconstructions from the memories of others. Thus, our memories of significant places are not impermeable, stable, or necessarily even factual. That ephemeral California exists only on Didion's private, internal map constructed of memory and longing; however, her private geography counteracts the pervasive placelessness and unsettledness which define the twentieth-century human condition.

Other American locations, too, do not exist for Didion, ultimately, as concrete places. Many of her essays, ostensibly about other issues, are actually portraits of cities in which they become narratives, stories, or ideas. Los Angeles was "literally invented by the *Los Angeles Times* and by its owners" ("Times Mirror Square," *AH* 222); the city is a "cloud" (*AH* 226), evolving as it did "not from the circumstances of geography but from sheer will, from an idea" (*AH* 248). Sections of Los Angeles are "Hammett and Chandler" ("7000 Romaine, Los Angeles 38," *STB* 78) country, a real landscape defined in terms of a more vivid and real fictional world. Las Vegas "exists only in the eye of the beholder" ("Marrying Absurd," *STB* 91); a city with "no sense of time," it offers "no logical sense of where one is" (*STB* 90). It exists detached, unconnected to "real" life; it lacks geographical or "historical imperative" (*STB* 91). There are three Hawaiis, according to Didion: the one on the atlas as of December 7, 1941; "a big rock candy mountain in the Pacific," the paradisiacal land of tourists; and a land associated with "the past, and with loss," the new American western frontier associated with World War II and the Vietnam War (*STB* 189–90). In "Goodbye to All That," Didion remembers the New York City of her early writing career not as a city of places but of "abstractions" embedded in her memory as a set of personal and professional moral lessons (*STB* 230). In her political writings about the Caribbean, places are insubstantial in the tropical air: in Miami "surfaces [tend] to dissolve," and "a certain liquidity suffuse[s] everything about the place" (*Miami* 36, 31). The city of Miami intertwines other narratives of the imagination to create its own: it "seem[s] not a city at all but a tale, a romance of the tropics, a kind of waking dream in which any possibility could and would be accommodated" (*Miami* 33).

In an effort to find order, Didion suggests, we must translate cities into forms that offer us the remote chance of constructing meaning, a logical narrative, what Didion repeatedly calls a "parable" ("Girl of the Golden West," *AH* 96). Her writing often conveys, like Hellman's, a moral edge that reinforces a code that could easily be labeled traditional American values and responsible individualism. Her long essay "Sentimental Journeys," apparently about the Central Park rape in April 1989, is not so much a story about the high-profile "wilding" incident, in which a female stock-broker was gang-raped by roaming male adolescents, as it is a portrait of New York City's inner landscape, the mindset necessary to survive in the most urban of American cities. The result is Didion's incisive examination of the city's numbness and indifference, as well as its consequent extremely high rate of violent crime.

She uses a similar pattern in her essay "Trouble in Lakewood"; ultimately, the place she portrays is a state of mind, one which breeds the likes of the infamous Spur Posse, a group of male suburban middle-class adolescents of unparalleled arrogance accused of numerous counts of sexual assault on underage girls. Behind the bright suburban landscape of Lakewood, the prototype of the post–World War II subdivisions that conveniently drew on the population boom to feed the aerospace industry, Didion discovers a moral chaos masquerading as the American dream. Complete with lifestyle and ideology, Lakewood and other models of the middle-class American Dream nurture a mentality that in fact isolates and alienates rather than promotes genuine community.

The title essay of *The White Album* encapsulates the threatening dissolution of the self *and* the fight to maintain a coherent identity—the security of the authoritative "I." Didion places in opposition two points of orientation on the map of self, one physical and one imaginary: her own body as primary, real geography and America as the cultural chaos that cannot be mapped in her writing. She establishes a connection between those two points of reference, the self and nation: "[A]n attack of vertigo and nausea does not now seem to me an inappropriate response to the summer of 1968" (15). With a devastating combination of journalistic objectivity and vulnerability, Didion parallels America's "falling apart" in the cultural upheaval of the 1960s and 1970s with her own "falling apart" following the onset of a nervous disorder. Her body, she insists, "was offering a precise physiological equivalent to what had been going on in [her] mind" (47). Her condition is "another story without a narrative" (47). In this stunning analogy, Didion aligns herself with her nation and conflates her own deterioration and alienation, as her psychiatric report expresses it, with the "atomization" of America as a concrete, stable place or a cohesive ideology (*STB*, "Preface" 11). Even as she admits to her fear that writing is an irrelevant act, however, she still wants "to believe in the narrative and the narrative's intelligibility" (*WA* 13). She suggests the only salvation now possible lies in deciphering the electronic impulses, surrendering to the circuitry of meaning, and becoming part of the "image" and context that is the hologram we call America.

Didion offers answers to the questions haunting autobiography studies in twenty-first century America. How do we reconcile the power offered by technology, the collectivity offered by living "on the grid," "in the air," and "on the air," with the frightening and disorienting consequences? Does such collectivity render individual political power futile even as it counters alienation? Are we to believe that Stein's America is real? Is the sacred freedom and political power of the individual merely an old-fashioned comforting American myth that Hellman and others fight to keep alive? Is Shepard's submission to displacement and identity confusion the answer? Didion's work foregrounds the dilemma of how we define Americanism in an era of multiculturalism and displacement. To what degree does America define us and to what degree do we define America? Or, to state her implied question, do we create the hologram on air, or does it create us?

All four authors question the mythic dimensions undergirding the stable geographical and political reality we conveniently call America — the same America Didion labels a "hologram on air." The contention that place, like self, is a construct implies that there is no stable site for a subject position in the genre and purports to reveal our "naive attachment to a tangible reality" (Ferriss).

The autobiographical inquiries of Stein, Hellman, and Shepard point toward positive transformations in our conceptions of autobiography, identity, and America. Stein resolves her question Who confers identity? by reconciling the dual identities conferred upon her by literature and by herself. The scoundrel time attests that Hellman succeeds in proving that each person has the rights to claim ownership of her memory and elevate it to public truth. Her worries about America's failure to remember prefigure Didion's hologram, an America without context and continuity where information circulates endlessly but does not provide the logical narrative that makes the center hold. Shepard embraces the "galaxy" of selves concealed by the unitary self as he investigates the possibilities of identity. He is ambivalent about family and human connections, with all their divisions and contradictions, for unlike Hellman, for him history and memory offer not only salvation but chaos and fear.

But are these rethinkings of self ultimately a reinforcement of individualism or a threat to it? Is our relinquishment of the geographical and ideological certainty we nostalgically cling to the America of the twenty-first century? Must indeterminacy translate into irrelevance and alienation? Must we conceive of place as a geographical certainty, as Lutwack's "tyranny of place" (237)? Must we insist on the false dichotomies of freedom versus placelessness, connectedness versus alienation? Or, can we, like Stein, Hellman, Shepard, and Didion reconcile contradictory readings of our exterior and interior landscapes? These twentieth-century authors speak not only of American anxiety, but of the capacity for greater personal, political, and social power from the multiple locations on the hologram that is America.

Chapter Notes

Introduction

1. See Sacvan Bercovitch, *The Puritan Origins of the American Self*, p. 186.

2. There are several other striking parallels between Stein and Whitman. See, for example, Thomas G. Couser's "Of Time and Identity: Walt Whitman and Gertrude Stein as Autobiographers."

3. My phrase ownership of memory is a variation of the ownership of the self, as explained by Robert Elbaz: "The autobiographer always tells the story of a past and, within that past, the linear development of one's 'own existence': what belongs to the author alone (or is 'owned' by him), his 'individual life' which translates into 'the history of his personality' — a central core which is self-consistent throughout its history" (2).

4. Terry Eagleton defines "sub-text" in the sense I use it here, and later in regard to the subtexts in *Scoundrel Time* (e.g., the italicized sections added to the second editions of her memoirs in *Three*, and the alternate versions of her HUAC statement left unsaid until the publication of *Scoundrel Time*) as "a text which runs within [the text], visible at certain 'symptomatic' points of ambiguity, evasion or overemphasis, and which we as readers are able to 'write' even if the novel itself does not.... The work's insights, as with all writing, are deeply related to its blindnesses: what it does not say, and *how* it does not say it, may be as important as what it articulates; what seems absent, marginal or ambivalent about it may provide a central clue to its meanings" (178).

5. Leigh Gilmore discusses another contemporary instance of this phenomenon, the "censure" Hannah Tillich experienced upon writing the biography of her husband, theologian Paul Tillich (*Autobiographics* 51). This case contains significant parallels to the anger and moralistic outcry after the publication of *Scoundrel Time*.

6. Bella Brodzki and Celeste Schenck note that this subjectivity is what "[Roland] Barthes' project arguably offers to a feminist reading of autobiography" (6).

Chapter One

1. Of particular note are the following studies: Shari Benstock's *The Private Self: Theory and Practice of Women's Autobiographical Writings*; Leigh Gilmore's *Autobiographics: A Feminist Theory of Women's Self-Representation*; Felicity Nussbaum's *The Autobiographical Subject: Gender and Ideology in Eighteenth-Century England*; Sidonie Smith's *A Poetics of Women's Autobiography: Marginality and the Fictions of Self-Representation*; and *Autobiography and Postmodernism*, edited by Kathleen Ashley, Leigh Gilmore, and Gerald Peters. Useful sources on the scope of autobiographical studies since 1960 include *Autobiography: Essays Theoretical and Critical*, edited by James Olney; Paul John Eakin's *Fictions in Autobiography: Studies in the Art of Self-Invention*; and John Paul Russo's "The Disappearance of the Self: Some Theories of Autobiography in the United States, 1964–1987." See Timothy Dow Adams' introduction to *Telling Lies in Modern American Autobiography* for a comprehensive overview of the state of American autobiographical studies as of 1990, with particular emphasis on the issue of fact versus fiction; and his "Introduction: Life Writing and Light Writing; Autobiography and Photography" (special issue of *Modern Fiction Studies*) for focus on the connections between autobiography and photography.

2. Sidonie Smith explains the double positioning of the subject: "Each of us is subject to and subject of discursive fields with universalizing, hegemonic tendencies…. Inside these webs, the subject is subjected as a passive, overdetermined pawn of large forces." However, "as heteronomous subjects, we are also active participants" ("Self" 15–16).

3. Kirby speculates on the emergence of this trend: "Space, then, seems to offer a medium for articulating — speaking and intertwining — the many facets, or phases, of subjectivity that have interested different kinds of theory: national origin, geographic and territorial mobility (deter-

mined by class, gender, and race), bodily presence and limits, structures of consciousness, and ideological formations of belonging and exclusion" (174). Kirby, unlike some theorists, carefully differentiates between place and space, as in her analysis of the similarities between Adrienne Rich's and Chandra Mohanty's space of the subject: "If place is organic and stable, space is malleable, a fabric of continually shifting sites and boundaries" (176). The advantage of the term *space* is that it avoids the seeming contradictions of "site" versus "plurality."

4. Other theorists have argued for the potential personal, political, and social power located in the subject. Paul Smith argues for a "human agent" that "exceeds" the subject and does not "foreclose upon the possibility of resistance" (xxx–xxxi). See Teresa de Lauretis for a definition of "a more useful conception of the subject than the one proposed by neo–Freudian psychoanalysis and poststructuralist theories" (9). She sees in the feminist redefining of the subject "a new aesthetic, a rewriting of culture" (10).

5. Fuss defines "the question of 'the body'" for the essentialist and the contructionist: "For the essentialist, the body occupies a pure, presocial, pre-discursive space ... is 'real,' accessible, and transparent.... For the constructionist, the body is never simply there, rather it is composed of a network of effects continually subject to sociopolitical determination. The body is 'always already' culturally mapped; it never exists in a pure or uncoded state" (5–6).

6. See Tuan for a comprehensive list of "recent publications [that] suggest a growing interest in the study of 'place' from a variety of humanistic perspectives" (207; note 3).

7. It is interesting to contrast the pessimistic and optimistic theories about postmodernism's influence on how we conceive of place, space, and subjectivity, and about the current interest in place/space. Kennedy suggests that "perhaps criticism and theory have now turned to the question of place in response to a growing suspicion that the inhuman landscape of postmodernism makes us all displaced persons by denying the grounding which would allow us to locate and define our lives" (*Imagining* xii). Conversely, Kirby notes "the *optimism* and anxiety of space in relation to identity in the modern, or postmodern, world" (175; emphasis added). Also, see note 5 above.

8. See Tuan for further discussion on the differences between space and place (6, 54).

9. Examples of such studies include the following: Patrick Bryce Bjork's *The Novels of Toni Morrison: The Search for Self and Place Within the Community*; Melvin Dixon's *Ride Out the Wilderness: Geography and*

Identity in Afro-American Literature; Suzanne W. Jones' "Place, Perception, and Identity in *The Awakening*"; and Peggy Nightingale's *A Sense of Place in the New Literatures in English*.

10. Trevor J. Barnes and James S. Duncan emphasize the similarities between texts and maps: maps are "susceptible to deconstruction," are "rhetorical devices used in cartographic communication," and possess an "inherent intertextuality." Barnes and Duncan postulate that cartography "normalizes and disciplines the world and as such is a part of the power/knowledge matrix" (17).

11. Shari Benstock describes the illusion that is the traditional auto-biographical text: "[T]he fabric of the narrative appears seamless, spun of whole cloth. The effect is magical—the self appears organic, the present the sum total of the past, the past an accurate predictor of the future" ("Authorizing" 19).

Chapter Two

1. James Breslin concludes that "the autobiographical act is one at odds with, even a betrayal of, Gertrude Stein's aesthetic principles" (149). I would modify the statement to say *at odds with traditional autobiography*. Trying to invent a narrative of the continuous present in all her writings, Stein sought an escape from memory and thus from an identity necessarily constructed on memory. By denying identity its unifying function, Stein (like Roland Barthes in his autobiographical work *Roland Barthes*) "resists the lure of both an idealized past and the idea that there is an 'other' self residing there, so that a prior period of self-unification can never stand as its subject's goal" (Paul Jay, "Being" 1057).

2. This concept parallels Stein's views on the opposition between the human mind and human nature, as explained by Ulla Dydo: "Her distinction, in *The Geographical History*, between the human mind, which is the source of creation, and human nature, which is merely the source of personality, is one result of the preoccupation with fame" (*Stein Reader* 588).

3. The openings to *Paris France* and *Wars I Have Seen* both regard expatriation to France in terms of a return to a place where she spent "a year when [she] was four to five" (*PF* 2). Her observation in *Wars* emphasizes the familiarity, not the strangeness, of her land of exile: "[O]ne of the things that seemed to me in 1914 was that Paris was then the way I remembered it when I was four only then there was not war" (5).

4. See J. Gerald Kennedy on how "encoded landscape figures in the operation of memory" ("Place" 505).

5. Linda Wagner-Martin suggests that the origin of this anxiety may rest with Stein's older sister, Bertha: "Bertha liked to tease Leo and Gertrude that they would not have been born had the other two children not died (a situation that made the two youngest Steins uncomfortable)" (*"Favored Strangers"* 13).

6. Here Stein refers to a Jewish custom that, in essence, effects the continuation of one identity when the first letter of the first name of an adult is "inherited" by a child. Evidently, Stein interpreted this custom to mean that the newborn child's separate identity is subsumed, at least in part, by a previously established one.

An intense examination of Stein's unorthodox sense of Jewishness has been provoked by the recent attacks on Stein for alleged participation in the Vichy government. Maria Damon argues that Stein "enacted and affirmed a kind of Jewishness that eschewed fixed categories and unlinear ways of thinking" (qtd. in Heller A16).

7. However, Elizabeth Winston, an exception, compares Stein's voice in *Everybody's Autobiography* to *The Making of Americans* and declares it "a striking advance in authorial confidence" (246).

8. In *Paris France*, Stein compares the scales of change Paris and America underwent in the first part of the twentieth century: "From 1900 to 1930, Paris did change a lot. They always told me that America changed but it really did not change as much as Paris did in those years that is the Paris that one can see, but then there is no remembering what it looked like before and even no remembering what it looks like now" (15).

9. The trauma evoked when one visits a place associated with a repressed episode "suggests ... that one's sense of place is determined less by specific geographical features than by experiential associations" (Kennedy, "Place" 499).

10. Stein mirrors the change identified by Arnold Krupat: "[T]he autobiographer's concept of writing" that developed from Benjamin Franklin to Henry David Thoreau was a move from "representation to creation," accompanied by a shift in emphasis from "the historicist component ... to ... egocentric individualism" (309).

11. Stein defines narration as "what was happening" (*EA* 302). In many ways, her approach to autobiography and narrative automatically rejects widely held assumptions about the mandatory correlation between autobiography and other narrative forms. See, for example, Pascal's insistence that autobiography exhibit the coherence of traditional narrative:

"The numberless impulses and responses of a person have to be reduced to a main strand" (185), and "[a]ll autobiographies must, like novels, have a story-structure" (187). Such views originate from an unquestioned belief in metaphysical selfhood, whereas Stein's autobiographical enterprises question that integral identity.

At odds with Stein's statement that "Anyway autobiography is easy like it or not autobiography is easy for any one" (*EA* 6), Pascal unwittingly reveals the major difference in his and Stein's views on autobiography. By insisting that "[t]rue autobiography can be written only by men and women pledged to their innermost selves" (195), he assumes that the self equals a stable, knowable essence. The autobiographer's task is "to give that unique truth of life as it is seen from inside" (195). He defines autobiography as a narrative, "a coherent shaping of the past" (5), and "something of a unity ... that may be reduced to order" (9), thereby assigning to the autobiographer the role of creator of an exterior self (what Stein disparagingly calls identity)—a self which has nothing to do with the writer's subjective view of the self.

12. She openly refuses to fabricate the organic wholeness we expect from traditional autobiography. Many critics have pointed out that *The Autobiography of Alice B. Toklas* achieves a similar anti-chronology, particularly because of the function of the photographs. The most notable of the photographs is the one following the final page of the book, an image of the first page of the handwritten manuscript of the same text. This image returns the reader to the beginning of the text.

13. The introduction remains unlabeled except in the table of contents and thus invites the reader to assign a title and function to the section (e.g., "Preface" or "Introduction"). It is unclear whether Stein or the editor assigned the label "Introduction" to this opening section.

14. Spengemann and Lundquist divide American autobiographers into several "cultural types": "prophets," "heroes," and "outsiders," each of which is defined less in terms of its attitude towards the self than how the type preserves, ignores, or challenges societal values.

15. The double voicedness and alternating pronouns emphasize the significant differences between the autobiographical projects of *The Autobiography* and *Everybody's Autobiography*, despite the fact that they are often assumed to be a natural pair. Very little criticism analyzes the vast differences between them. Terms such as Lynn Z. Bloom's "autobiography-by-*Doppelgänger*" and "ventriloquistic persona" ("Gertrude" 82, 83) label, for example, two unique attributes of *The Autobiography* that are not applicable to *Everybody's Autobiography*.

16. Lejeune's discussion of alternating pronouns centers on the first-

and third-person forms; however, the dynamic he describes is relevant to Stein's use of the singular and plural first-person pronouns. "We" is not only ambiguous but evasive.

17. Stein also alternated between the pronouns in later texts, though often inconsistently and seemingly arbitrarily. In *Paris France*, for example, she often shifts from "I" to "we"; the texts, however, do not present this pronoun shifting as an enigma (i.e., this shifting, less puzzling than that in Stein's later work, has not been the topic of numerous critical articles, as has the pronoun shifting and confusion in *The Autobiography*). It is very clear that "we" refers to Alice B. Toklas and herself.

18. However, this is not true of later texts, such as *Wars I Have Seen*, in which the very focus of the book is her and Toklas's experiences in World War II.

19. See Shari Benstock's *Women of the Left Bank* for a discussion of this frightening riot of February 6, 1934, that "nearly resulted in a Fascist coup d'etat" (127–28).

20. See Wagner-Martin's *"Favored Strangers"* for evidence, corroborated by several Stein siblings, that there was ample reason to harbor resentment toward the Stein patriarch. Daniel Stein often behaved in an angry and threatening way, thereby controlling his wife and children (7, 13, 17). He exacted physical punishment on Stein (and possibly Bertha as well) (xiii, 26), and Stein's writings also suggest that he attempted to sexually abuse his daughters (25).

21. For an analysis of Stein's seeming "indifference" that denied the "centrality of her mother," see Wagner-Martin, *"Favored Strangers,"* pp. 20–22. The years between the onset of her mother's illness and her father's death spanned much of Stein's adolescence (age eleven to just several weeks before her seventeenth birthday); those years she was preoccupied with death. Stein writes of that time, "It was when I was between twelve and seventeen that I went through the dark and dreadful days of adolescence, in which predominated the fear of death, not so much of death as of dissolution, and naturally is war like that" (*WIHS* 14).

See Lisa Ruddick for insightful comments on Stein's feelings about her mother. Writing of the period after Alice B. Toklas became Stein's "primary companion" (1912–13) and Leo Stein absented himself from her life (181), Ruddick observes that Stein's "works ... bespeak a wandering toward the mother" (182). Toklas "repaired certain emotional wounds that had previously made maternal themes unsafe for Stein" (183). Ruddick speculates that Stein had felt "insulted" knowing that her birth was not planned and that she was second choice. In the dominant-submissive relationship with Toklas, Stein was "unconsciously taking revenge on her uninvolved mother" (185). In addition to being a "nonentity" (184), a fact which encouraged Stein to identify with her father, the mother was a "threatening model" for Stein because "identifying with her mother would mean dying as her mother had" (186). Clearly, Stein's preoccupation with her conception (evident in *Everybody's Autobiography* and texts written during the early Toklas years) suggests that the relationship with Toklas was not a "resolution of those deep maternal issues but a solution that on a superficial level worked" (185).

22. In *Paris France*, Stein declares, "Paris was where the twentieth century was" (11), implying either that she, being a genius of the twentieth century, was compelled to live in Paris, or that the twentieth century took place in Paris simply due to her presence there. Naturalizing her choice to expatriate, she says, "So Paris was the place that suited those of us that were to create the twentieth century art and literature, naturally enough," and "[s]o the twentieth century did need France as a background" (*PF* 12, 106). Stein imagines World War II to be a kind of coming-of-age for America, at war's closing declaring her native country to be "the oldest country in the world" because "she was the first country to enter into the twentieth century" (*WIHS* 257).

Stein also comments in *Wars I Have Seen* on the impressive aerial view of America in a way that equates it with a vast canvas on whose surface humans draw or create America: "And when you think how ruled the lines are of the states, no natural boundaries of mountains or rivers but just ruled out with a ruler to make lines and angles and all the same each one of the states has its own character, its own accent, just like provinces in France which are so ancient" (250).

23. Stein's comment on William James' definition of science suggests a source for her unique logic that seems to equate observation with truth: "[William James] ... said science is not a solution and not a problem it is a statement of the observation of things observed and perhaps therefore not interesting perhaps therefore only abjectly true" (*EA* 242). Do Stein or James doubt that science may be interesting and "perhaps ... only abjectly true"? It is unclear how much of the statement is Stein's and how much is James', or if their opinions overlap.

Furthermore, Shirley Neuman argues that Stein "modifies the techniques of scientific observation to serve her atemporal literature" (*Narration* 48). She justifies her subjective convictions by means of "the scientific paradigm" in her narrative (*Narration* 53).

24. A series of essays following her American tour points to her preoccupation with defining the American character.

Chapter Three

1. Martha Gellhorn's violent response to Hellman's style of memoir ("On Apocryphism") serves as but one example of the clash between the view that facts (truth) and fiction utterly exclude one another, and the view that truth often escapes fact: "Miss Hellman is the very devil to pin down on dates which is peculiar in non-fiction where facts and dates are essentially linked" (288). Although she dismisses Hellman as an incompetent on what might be argued are sometimes trivial points (e.g., inaccurate details about European train schedules in 1939, as recorded in *Pentimento*), Gellhorn's principal complaint centers on the ownership of the Hemingway legend, her revision of it, and her defense of his image against the likes of Stephen Spender and Hellman. Ironically, Gellhorn lambastes them for the very thing she does herself: insists on the authenticity of her memories of Hemingway over the memories of others.

2. In "Arthur W. A. Cowan" in *Pentimento*, Hellman mentions her reluctance to write about that period: "I had already learned that I could not, did not wish to explain, or be wise about, or handle the bitter storm that the McCarthy period caused, causes, in me" (524). In a 1974 interview with Bill Moyers, she explains that writing about what Moyers calls her politics "seems to be something that at least at this period of my life I can't do" (Bryer 153). Timothy Dow Adams speculates that Richard Nixon was "the stimulus" for her writing *Scoundrel Time* (*Telling* 153), and Carl Rollyson attributes the writing of *Scoundrel Time* to "the pressure of the times and of her own participation in the Committee for Public Justice" (481), which filed suit against Nixon to force him to surrender the Watergate tapes as evidence.

The controversy provoked by Oliver Stone's film *Nixon* (1995) is a striking ironic parallel to Hellman's situation, for Stone duplicates Hellman's demand to present a personal version of truth that doubles as American history. Also, the film controversy reminds us of the Hellman-Nixon connection.

3. Hellman's appearance before HUAC was part of their lengthy investigation into possible Communist infiltration into the motion picture industry. For full information on HUAC's impact on Hollywood, see Navasky's chapter, "HUAC in Hollywood."

4. The collaboration with attorney Joseph Rauh reveals the strategic composition process that produced the letter: "Rauh wrote a letter that I was to send to the Committee; I didn't like it much because it didn't sound like me. Then I wrote a version, he wrote another, I rewrote him,

he rewrote me, and we came out with the version that I quote here"
(*ST* 658).

5. Hellman was frequently accused of bolstering her heroic status by
implying that she was the first to refuse to name names to HUAC. See Marilyn Berger's interview with Hellman (1979) for Hellman's clarifications
that (1) she certainly was not the first witness not to name names, (2) she
did not present herself in *Scoundrel Time* as "standing alone" in that refusal
[thus acknowledging the accusations of critics such as Sidney Hook (86)],
and (3) her position differed from that of many other witnesses only in
that she "tried not to take the Fifth Amendment" by offering to talk only
about herself, a position that in itself is "a violation of the Fifth Amendment" (252).

6. For two of the most scathing and well-known attacks on Hellman,
see William F. Buckley and Sidney Hook. Buckley's reference to Dashiell
Hammett as Hellman's "common-law husband" typifies the tone of his
vicious and personal assault (105). Timothy Dow Adams' section on
Scoundrel Time (pp. 153–62) provides not only an excellent and detailed
summary of the entire controversy, but insightfully offers a more even-
handed reading of the text that demands neither the reader's total admiration for nor rejection of Hellman.

7. This admirable attitude about the land echoes an ethic expressed
in Hellman's play *The Little Foxes*. In a 1968 interview, she explains: "I certainly meant something by it [*The Little Foxes*, 1939] in an over-all social
sense — that it was a sin to see beautiful land go in a bad way, a bad way
for me" (Funke in Bryer 101). Hellman and Hammett's refusal to sell the
farm to "someone who would subdivide it and build a lot of houses" dramatically illustrates their idealism about not spoiling the land. Oddly,
though, Hellman seems to regret partially her decision to go along with
Hammett; she sold the land "for nothing" and had mixed feelings about
Hammett's decision. She felt "rather proud and very angry" (a confusing
statement she doesn't clarify) that she and Hammett did not benefit finan-
cially from land that in later years was sub-divided and spoiled by someone else anyway. See the Berger interview in Bryer, p. 260.

8. It is curious that critics have not rigorously exposed and debated
the obvious chronological discrepancies in this scene. I contend that the
significance of this scene has been overlooked because subjective,
unverifiable truth, unlike her politics, cannot easily be used to condemn
Hellman, and because exploring the motive for fudging the truth presents
complex genre issues.

9. However, some critics stress the importance of examining *Scoundrel Time* separately. For example, Marcus Billson and Sidonie Smith feel

that "the critical problems posed by the strategy of the 'other' [in *Scoundrel Time*] require a study in themselves," for "the reverberations of her public image" in *Scoundrel Time* constitute an "other" (178). But others stress the opposite. Timothy Dow Adams notes the importance of seeing the memoirs in context, as a whole; they act as pentimenti to one another (142). Linda Wagner-Martin differentiates between the first three memoirs and the fourth, the first three reflecting Hellman's sureness about her ability to accomplish her ends and the last expressing the inability to know oneself or another person (285).

10. Adams alone points out the other side of her heroics. Hellman herself mocks "her lifelong habit of taking the romantic moral stance" (121). Rigid and overly judgmental critics have also failed to see that she de-emphasizes a heroic role created in part by her reading public. She regrets more than once that she "didn't have the nerve" to say what she really wanted to say to the committee and walk out (Berger in Bryer 249). She gives much credit to her legal counsel for her decision to offer to speak of herself in the letter to Wood: "And it was actually *not my idea*. It was the idea of the very brilliant Abe Fortas, and was carried out, not only with the able ... but with the thoughtfulness of the very famous Joseph Rauh. But they were very worried I was going to get very nervous about my going to jail on it. They had no legal grounds to stand on.... There were *no heroics* about it one way or the other. The heroics have been thought up by people who don't like me" (Berger in Bryer 252–53; emphasis added).

11. I cannot, however, condone Kramer's attack on Hellman and Dashiell Hammett following Hellman's death. He deplores her decision to leave much of her estate to the creation of a Dashiell Hammett Fund that "will make grants 'for the promotion and advancement of political, social and economic equality, civil right and civil liberties'" (5). (Hellman/Hammett Grants are awarded annually by Human Rights Watch/Free Expression Project, formerly the Fund for Free Expression, to "writers for their courage in the face of political persecution" ["Human Rights Watch"].) Kramer asserts that: "In bequeathing so large a portion of her wealth to a fund honoring the *beliefs* of yet another unrepentant Stalinist, Lillian Hellman wrote her own truest epitaph" (6). Kramer's comment exemplifies the length to which Hellman's critics will go (even after her death) to turn any sign of Hellman's liberal politics — even one as admirable as this — into an occasion for personal attack.

12. Hellman told Rex Reed in 1975 that "[a] psychiatrist [Gregory Zilboorg] once told me something very revealing about myself. I was too young to understand what he meant at the time, but now I see the insight. He said I look at myself as though I'm a total stranger" (Bryer 181). She

elaborates on her objectivity about herself in 1976: "The man who ana-
lyzed me once said I was the only patient he'd ever had in his life who
talked about herself as if I were another person. He meant no compli-
ment. He meant that I had too cold a view of myself" (Doudna in Bryer
201).

13. Hellman's comment on her play *The Autumn Garden*, in 1951,
gives an early indication of how crucial she felt inner character or morality was to a person's resiliency: "Perhaps, in the play, I've wanted to say
that if you've had something to stand on inwardly when you reach the middle years you have a chance of being all right; if you haven't you just live
out your life" (Morehouse in Bryer 23). Adams on Hellman's absolutist
view of character: "Lillian Hellman's emphasis on honor over identity as
something one either has or does not have reflects her basic orientation
toward moral issues" (122).

14. Interestingly, this accusation against HUAC foreshadows (or duplicates, since she did not finally have her say until 1975) the self-accusation
that she used other people's lives for self-aggrandizement. The identity of
Julia is the definitive example. See Hellman's italicized comments in *Three*,
pp. 449–52, and Rollyson, pp. 514–28, for a summary of the controversy.

15. This 1978 tribute indicates that in her later years Hellman gained
perspective on just how influential Hammett was in her becoming a successful writer: "His effect on me was enormous. I've long had a belief,
which is very possibly not the truth, that, without Hammett, I wouldn't
have written. I've come to think, perhaps, that I would have written, but
I would have had an infinitely greater struggle, and been less good, I think
without him. ... There was a time when I thought that I would never have
written anything without him. I don't think that's true any more. But I
think I would have had a much harder time, so hard that I might have given
up" (Adam in Bryer 225).

16. In chapter 6 of *An Unfinished Woman*, Hellman describes that
dangerous time in Hollywood after her marriage to Arthur Kober and
before meeting Hammett — her lack of direction, depression, dissatisfac-
tion with her job reading manuscripts at MGM, and her failing marriage.
Her mood and attitude toward the urban landscape anticipates Shepard's:

> [T]he drive [home at six o'clock] had become so bad for me that
> I would tremble as I got into the car and would often have to stop the
> car and press my hands together to stop the movements they were
> making. Sometimes when I stopped I fell asleep for a while; once
> I leaned from the window and screamed; once I left the car, went to
> a small hotel and phoned to say I couldn't get home and didn't want
> anybody to come for me; twice I had minor accidents and once I

killed a rabbit and sat by it for a few hours. I did not yet know about "inhuman cities" or roads built with no relief for the eye, or the effects of a hated house upon the spirit. I didn't even understand about my marriage, or my life, and had no knowledge of the new twists I was braiding into the kinks I was already bound round with. (*UW* 70)

Hellman says in *An Unfinished Woman*, "We [she and Hammett] met when I was twenty-four years old and he was thirty-six in a restaurant in Hollywood" (278). Rollyson, however, puts Hellman's age at twenty-five when she met Hammett in Fall 1930 (41).

17. Joan Mellen's 1996 biography, *Hellman and Hammett*, takes a particularly negative and cynical view of their relationship—a view much noted by reviewers. Stacey D'Erasmo comments on Mellen's biography: "For Mellen, the question is: How did Hellman manage to steal so much of Hammett's identity without anyone noticing, and secondarily, why was she so ugly? Hellman, in Mellen's view, was some sort of Succubus, filled with rage about her looks, who absorbed Hammett—his literary gifts, his politics, his alcoholism, his sexual appetite, even his manner of speaking—in a fury of unrequited love" (25–26).

18. The loss of Sophronia and Hellman's replacement of her with Helen provide a feminine parallel to Hammett as a male icon: "Oh, Sophronia, it's you I want back always. It's by you I still so often measure, guess, transmute, translate and act" (*UW* 255). Connections might also be made between Hammett, Sophronia, and Hellman's father. Hellman's father called Sophronia "the only control [Hellman] ever recognized" (*UW* 24). In her adulthood, Hellman transferred that recognition to Hammett. Bernard Benstock points out the remarkable, perhaps unconscious, resemblance for Hellman between her father and Hammett (20).

19. See *An Unfinished Woman*, pp. 212–13, for an example of the self-destructive "game that men and women play against each other." Hellman's comment on Hammett's reaction after reading the eighth version of *The Little Foxes* reveals her dependence on his semi-sadistic manner of criticizing her work, even though she honestly admired and depended on him as a literary critic (*P* 474–75). Hellman's account of her breathless wait for Hammett's reaction to *The Autumn Garden* typifies the mixture of nervousness, dependence, and admiration in their writer-critic relationship (*UW* 287–88).

20. Hellman's Jewish heritage is strangely absent from her strident co-opting of the glittering generalities of America's Protestant-based New England ethos. For all her moralizing, she expresses some ambivalence about her Jewish roots, Puritanism, and religion in general. Questioned about her Jewishness in the 1970s, Hellman admitted that it was part of

her identity, but that she did not really understand what it meant to her: "I would rather be a Jew than not be. I think Nazism had a great deal to do with that. It suddenly became very important to me" (Doudna in Bryer 197). Just three years before her death, she maintains her sense of Jewishness as more of a cultural than a religious influence: "I wasn't brought up as a Jew. I know almost nothing about being one — I'm sorry to say — though not sorry enough to go to the trouble of learning.... Whether brought up as one or not, somewhere in the background there was a gift of being born a Jew. I don't want it to alter my point of view about things any more than I would want being Catholic or anything else to alter my point of view, but I am glad of what I am" (Drake in Bryer 291). For a discussion of Hellman's supposed anti–Semitic tendencies, arguably discredited by the above comments, see Rollyson's chapter on *Scoundrel Time*.

In another interview, she claims not to know what the words *Puritan* or *religion* mean. Perhaps her mother's habit of visiting any church that was convenient, regardless of denomination, instilled in Hellman in childhood her sense of religion as an amalgamation of spiritual and moral views ultimately validated by one's personal experience and sense of decency rather than by an institution.

21. Hellman filed a libel suit in early 1980 against Mary McCarthy for $2.25 million in damages for being called a liar on *The Dick Cavett Show*. The suit was pending at the time of Hellman's death in 1984. See Adams, p. 121, and Rollyson, p. 512.

Chapter Four

1. See Gary Grant for a discussion of Shepard's remarkable "sensitivity to place" (554).

2. In Michael VerMeulen's *Esquire* article in February 1980, Shepard comments on his familial happiness and contrasts it to his lifelong anxiety over feeling lost: "I feel like I've never had a home, you know?" Interestingly, he speculates that the "real home" is in the "recognition of each other," the intimacy discovered in people, not in place (86).

3. Shepard joined organizer Bob Dylan, Allen Ginsberg, Joan Baez, and numerous other artists in 1976 for the rock tour the Rolling Thunder Revue. Dylan hired Shepard to write the screenplay for the film version of the tour. The film never materialized, but he did publish his account in *The Rolling Thunder Logbook*.

4. Relph points out the differences between "the old road" and "the new road" associated with placelessness. The old road "was a definite place,

a strip of land that went between other places"; it "encouraged social contact" and "involv[ed] the traveler directly in the landscape." The new road, "an essentially twentieth century creation and an extension of man's vehicle, ... does not connect places nor does it link with the surrounding landscape." The "primary requirement" of the new road is "that it start from where the people are and go on indefinitely, not that it go between places or lead to places"; it "starts everywhere and leads nowhere" (90). William Q. Boelhower sums up twentieth-century mobility: "Everybody is officially on the road, looking for a better place to live" (119).

Leonard Lutwack's prediction emphasizes the importance of the automobile and its link to a sense of "home": "A moving place — automobile, van, spacecraft — may be the nest for people of the twentieth and twenty-first centuries" (37). Even an object, if it is an "inhabitable space" (27), can qualify as a place. Thus even home, the most static and stable of places, the haven of emotional and physical security, becomes mobilized.

5. The spiritual aspects discernible in Shepard's attitude about being "on the road" echo, for example, these passages from Whitman's "Song of the Open Road": "Afoot and light-hearted I take to the open road, / Healthy, free, the world before me, / The long brown path before me leading wherever I choose" (ll. 1–3); and "O public road, ... I am not afraid to leave you, yet I love you, / You express me better than I can express myself, / You shall be more to me than my poem" (ll. 46–48).

6. Patti Smith, a close friend of Shepard's, in "9 Random Years [7 + 2]" characterizes him as constantly on the road and even documents all the cars he owned. In portraying his natural state as "on the road," she sheds light on Shepard's preoccupation with artists who died in car accidents — James Dean and Jackson Pollock, to name a representative two. He often pays indirect tributes in his plays to self-destructive, alienated artists (e.g., Johnny Ace in *Cowboy Mouth*). George Stambolian has also noted this obsession and offers an explanation: "He believes that these deaths, whether accidental or the results of suicide, reveal the deep frustrations of life in America that success intensifies by imposing an image on the artist that alienates him from himself and others" (87).

7. Don Shewey aptly sums up the spiritual-geographical metaphor in Shepard's work in a comment on the play *True West*: "The true West is in the mind. No, the true West is in the soul" (*Sam Shepard* 140).

8. "In Shepard's plays, the 'frontier' symbolizes those open spaces where law, order, and social restrictions [i.e., civilization, history] have never invaded and primitive longings for individual power gain prompt release" (Falk 91).

9. In her 1993 interview with Shepard, Carol Rosen remarked to

Shepard, "You don't see America the way an American does. You step away from it and look at it from a distance." She compared his view of America to that of Wim Wenders, the German filmmaker. Shepard explained the objectivity that living outside a country gives by replying that Europeans have a "critical eye" that Americans lack, and that "for the most part, ... Americans have lost the compassion for their own country" (9).

10. Jesse Mojo, O-Lan Johnson and Shepard's son and only child, was born in 1970. He and Lange named their first son and second child Samuel in 1987. Shepard's renewal of the father's lineage suggests a reconciliation between emotional connectedness and "possibility" (See note 12). According to Don Shewey, O-Lan Johnson Shepard "continues to subsidize" Overtone Industries as actress O-Lan Jones. She originally founded the production company in San Francisco and "took it with her when she relocated to Los Angeles" ("Identity Dance" 14).

11. Ron Mottram notes that "Curse [of the Starving Class] generalizes its subjects by using the condition of the family as a metaphor for the human condition itself, which dooms everyone to be a carrier and transmitter of the poisons of past generations" (132). Many Shepard plays, particularly the others in the family trilogy, Buried Child and True West, deal with the opposing forces contained in inheritance and bloodties. In a 1993 interview Shepard spoke of character as "an essential tendency ... that can't be ultimately changed. It's like the structure of our bones, the blood that runs through our veins" (Rosen 8). Here he suggests a solidity and permanence to individual identity, as inherited from the family, that his earlier writings do not reflect.

12. Shepard's comments on his relationship with Jessica Lange define his sense of "possibility": "I would have been down the river if I hadn't met Jessica.... There was salvation for me. It's just this suddenly being connected with someone in a way you never knew was possible. It's like a revelation.... And in this case for me it has to do with love and the possibility of a real family" (Kroll 74).

Interestingly, shortly before his breakup with O-Lan Johnson, Shepard felt he was "closer to happiness ... than he [had] ever been before" (VerMeulen 86), because of his family life, successful work, and resettlement in California.

13. Another quite different version of Shepard's birth appears in Hawk Moon; Mottram contrasts the two versions and concludes that the version in Hawk Moon, based on Hopi Indian ritual, offers "membership in a stable and satisfying community that fully defines the role and place of the individual" (2).

14. Leonard Lutwack explains "the age-old ambivalence of man's

view of his earthly abode": (1) "that earth is a hostile, alien place, keeping man from a human potential that can only be realized by transcending earth" and (2) "that earth is man's true home, his only possible environment, which he must adapt to and control in order to fulfill himself" (3).

15. Shepard repeatedly identifies his father with warplanes. Sam Sr., a bomber pilot in World War II, maintained a reverence for planes. Each time he hears a plane go overhead, he "squint[s] deep into the sky" and picks at an old shrapnel scar on the back of his neck (118).

16. Mottram states that "a longing for the father" (46) runs through Shepard's work. Doris Auerbach optimistically suggests that "even more than an acceptance from a father, [Shepard's protagonists] are searching for a mother whose nurturance would make the world fruitful again" (8). Several critics lambaste Shepard for failing to portray female characters with emotional dimension. In two of his midlife works, specifically *Fool for Love* (1983) and *A Lie of the Mind* (1986), Shepard answers Auerbach's optimism. He portrays May and Beth, in *Fool* and *Lie* respectively, with sensitivity and insight. In 1993, when questioned about the possibly "feminist" point of view in some of his plays, Shepard commented on "the female side of things": "You know, in yourself, that the female part of one's self as a man is, for the most part, battered and beaten up and kicked to shit just like some women in relationships. That men themselves batter their own female part to their own detriment. And it became interesting from that angle: as a man what is it like to embrace the female part of yourself that you historically damaged for one reason or another" (Rosen 6–7).

17. Sam Sr. resembles the fictional fathers in Shepard's plays (e.g., Jake's father in *A Lie of the Mind*, the father in *True West* who lives "destitute" in the desert and "drinks up" the money the writer son gives him (*Seven Plays* 33), and the wandering father of *Fool for Love*.

18. A scene in *Paris, Texas* clearly draws on this early memory: Travis and his estranged son Hunter make a phone call from a public phone with a dinosaur scene in the background.

19. Ironically, Shepard portrays a figure very similar to his father (complete with leather jacket) in *The Right Stuff*: Chuck Yeager, a full-fledged contemporary American hero. Perhaps it is significant that by the time of that filming, Sam Rogers, Sr., had died.

20. *A Lie of the Mind* (1986) draws on this experience; however, in the play, Beth's brain damage results from the violent beating caused by her jealous husband Jake. The play repeats the motif of the mother-father dichotomy but with intensified realism and violence.

21. Shepard's loss of a coherent identity around the time of Scarlett

Johnson's illness corresponds to Lacan's mirror stage, in which the child perceives the mother as an entity separate and no longer accessible to him. Thus, he is forced into the symbolic, the realm of the father.

22. Gary Grant speaks of this conflict between father and mother as reflected in Shepard's plays: "Shepard's intense observation of the self in his relationships with women seems to have unearthed a deep conflict between his consciousness of women and his consciousness of his father as a source of feelings of continuity and connection" (559).

23. David Wyatt notes that *Motel Chronicles* was originally entitled "Transfiction" or "Transfixion." He contends that "[b]y replacing the 'c' with the 'x', Shepard links fiction-making and suffering — writing becomes a kind of crucifixion" (355).

24. Gardiner cites as the alternative to this "repression" model Chodorow's "model of female *personality* formation" that is "cyclical," and "progressive." Gardiner expands this theory: "female identity is a process" (Gardiner 352–53).

25. Boelhower draws the parallel between American westward expansion and circularity: "According to the dynamics of the map, there was only one verb to express the process of building a homeland and it was an imperative: EXPAND! The history of the United States is nothing but a series of variations on this theme, to the point that an originally spatial concept, the West, was transformed into an abstract game of circulation" (73–74). Edward Relph attributes the "sameness" of the American landscape (e.g., identical Howard Johnson's restaurants in each state) to a "uniformity" that attempts to replace "the infinity of westward expansion with that of circularity" (114).

26. Shepard's story "Winging It" in *Cruising Paradise*, his 1996 collection of autobiographical writings, further explores the dilemma of effectively merging the "real" self with the character he is playing in a film.

27. Foucault defines *projection*: "These aspects of an individual which we designate as making him an author are only a projection, in more or less psychologizing terms, of the operations that we force texts to undergo, the connections that we make, the traits that we establish as pertinent, the continuities that we recognize, or the exclusions that we practice" (150). Shepard's spectrum of narrative stances challenges even a definition as all-encompassing as this.

28. The text-photograph pairs are as follows: (1) poem about "Poor Texas / Carved into / Like all the rest," with photograph of a small-town, western street; (2) narrative about friend who believes in the "Faraway Radioland" on the car radio, with photograph of Johnny Dark and Shepard wearing a cowboy hat, both men standing by a vintage car and truck

(circa 1940s or 1950s); (3) narrative in which Sam Sr. gives Shepard a tour of the pictures on the wall, with photograph of Shepard and Sam Sr. in a cowboy hat (apparently the same one Shepard wears in the "Poor Texas" photograph); (4) narrative about the four-day truck ride, with photograph of Johnny Dark in sunglasses, sitting on the front bumper of a large truck; (5) "natural woman" poem, with photograph of O-Lan Johnson sprawled across washer, dryer, and ironing board; (6) fragment about horse and horse's tail, with photograph of a large Mobil flying horse (Pegasus image) sign against a clear sky crossed by telephone wires; (7) narrative about Sam Sr.'s love for planes and his "habit of picking at a shrapnel scar on the back of his neck," with photograph of him and Shepard wearing a cowboy hat; (8) narrative about Shepard's impulse to leave the family, with an outdoor photograph of a large "family" group.

29. Many critics have noted the similar development of autobiography theory and photographic theory. See Timothy Dow Adams, "Introduction," and Lorraine M. York, for example.

30. André Bazin notes this paradoxical "objective character of photography" which gives it "a quality of credibility absent from all other picture making." However, he also notes that photography goes beyond supplying "a mere approximation," substitute, or reproduction; it is "the object itself" (241).

31. "In April 1982 Shepard and O-Lan took a trip to New Mexico with Scarlett and Johnny to visit Sam Sr.— a visit that probably formed the basis of a father-son encounter described in *Motel Chronicles*" (Shewey, *Sam Shepard* 147).

32. André Bazin's comments on the origins of and psychological needs met by painting and sculpture appropriately sum up the needs fulfilled by photography. In what Bazin calls "the mummy complex," the artist seeks to preserve the body against time and the inevitable decay it brings: "No one believes any longer in the ontological identity of model and image, but all are agreed that the image helps us to remember the subject and to preserve him from a second spiritual death" (238).

33. Ron Mottram explains this advantage in his comment on Crow's speech in *The Tooth of Crime*: "'I believe in my mask—The Man I made up is me / And I believe in my dance—And my destiny'." Unlike Hoss, who can switch voices because he does not believe that any of them are really his, Crow never switches voices because he believes that the one he projects is not a voice at all but is his true self. He believes in the mask he has created" (*Seven Plays* 106). This advantage, of course, allows Crow to destroy Hoss and inherit his empire.

34. For Aaron's account of both events, see Oumano, p. 46.

Works Cited
and Consulted

Adams, Timothy Dow. "Introduction: Life Writing and Light Writing; Autobiography and Photography." *Modern Fiction Studies* 40.3 (Fall 1994): 459–92.

_____. *Telling Lies in Modern American Autobiography*. Chapel Hill: University of North Carolina Press, 1990.

Ashley, Kathleen, Leigh Gilmore, and Gerald Peters, eds. *Autobiography and Postmodernism*. Amherst: University of Massachusetts Press, 1994.

Atlas, James. "The Age of the Literary Memoir Is Now." *New York Times Magazine* 12 May 1996: 25–27.

Auerbach, Doris. *Sam Shepard, Arthur Kopit, and the Off Broadway Theatre*. Boston: Twayne, 1982.

Barnes, Trevor J., and James S. Duncan, eds. *Writing Worlds: Discourse, Text and Metaphor in the Representation of Landscape*. New York: Routledge, 1992.

Barthes, Roland. *Camera Lucida: Reflections on Photography*. Trans. by Richard Howard. New York: Hill and Wang, 1981.

_____. "Rhetoric of the Image." Trachtenberg 269–85.

Baudrillard, Jean. *America*. Trans. by Chris Turner. New York: Verso, 1988.

Bazin, André. "The Ontology of the Photographic Image." Trachtenberg 237–44.

Benstock, Bernard. "Non-Negotiable Bonds: Lillian Hellman and Dashiell Hammett." Unpublished manuscript, 1991.

Benstock, Shari. "Authorizing the Autobiographical." Benstock, *Private Self* 10–33.

_____, ed. *The Private Self: Theory and Practice of Women's Autobiographical Writings*. Chapel Hill: University of North Carolina Press, 1988.

_____. *Women of the Left Bank*. Austin: University of Texas Press, 1986.

Bercovitch, Sacvan. *The Puritan Origins of the American Self*. New Haven, Conn.: Yale University Press, 1975.

Bergland, Betty. "Postmodernism and the Autobiographical Subject: Reconstructing the 'Other.'" Ashley 130–66.

Billson, Marcus K., and Sidonie A. Smith. "Lillian Hellman and the Strategy of the 'Other.'" Jelinek, *Women's Autobiography* 163–79.

Bjork, Patrick Bryce. *The Novels of Toni Morrison: The Search for Self and Place Within the Community*. New York: Peter Lang, 1992.

Blake, Nancy. *"Everybody's Autobiography: Identity and Absence." Recherches Anglaises et Americaines* 15 (1982): 135–45.

Blasing, Mutlu Konuk. *The Art of Life: Studies in American Autobiographical Literature*. Austin: University of Texas Press, 1977.

Bloom, Lynn Z. "Gertrude Is Alice Is Everybody: Innovation and Point of View in Gertrude Stein's Autobiographies." *Twentieth-Century Literature* 24.1 (Spring 1978): 81–93.

_____. "Lynn Bloom Replies." *a/b: Auto/Biography Studies* 4.1 (Fall 1988): 27.

_____. "Shaping Women's Lives." *a/b: Auto/Biography Studies* 4.1 (Fall 1988): 17–23.

_____. "Single-Experience Autobiographies." *a/b: Auto/Biography Studies* 3.3 (Fall 1987): 36–45.

Boelhower, William Q. *Through a Glass Darkly: Ethnic Semiosis in American Literature*. New York: Oxford University Press, 1987.

Brantley, Ben. "Sam Shepard, Storyteller." *New York Times* 13 Nov. 1994: 1H+.

Breslin, James E. "Gertrude Stein and the Problems of Autobiography." Jelinek, *Women's Autobiography* 149–62.

Brodzki, Bella, and Celeste Schenck. Introduction. *Life/Lines: Theorizing Women's Autobiography*. Eds. Bella Brodzki and Celeste Schenck. Ithaca N.Y.: Cornell University Press, 1988.

Broe, Mary Lynn, and Angela Ingram, eds. *Women's Writing in Exile*. Chapel Hill: University of North Carolina Press, 1989.

Brown, Maurice F. "Autobiography and Memory: The Case of Lillian Hellman." *Biography* 8.1 (Winter 1985): 1–11.

Bruss, Elizabeth W. *Autobiographical Acts: The Changing Situation of a Literary Genre*. Baltimore: Johns Hopkins University Press, 1976.

_____. "Eye for I: Making and Unmaking Autobiography in Film." Olney, *Autobiography* 296–320.

Bryer, Jackson R., ed. *Conversations with Lillian Hellman*. Literary Conversations Series. Jackson: University of Mississippi Press, 1986.

Buckley, William F., Jr. "*Scoundrel Time*: And Who Is the Ugliest of Them All?" *National Review* 29 (21 Jan. 1977): 101–06.

Canby, Vincent. "Sam Shepard's Aim Wavers in a Replay of 'Tooth of Crime.'" *New York Times* 12 Jan. 1997: H7+.

Couser, Thomas G. *American Autobiography: The Prophetic Mode*. Amherst: University of Massachusetts Press, 1979.

_____. "Of Time and Identity: Walt Whitman and Gertrude Stein as Autobiographers." *Texas Studies in Language and Literature* 17.4 (Winter 1976): 787–804.

Cox, James M. "Autobiography and America." *Aspects of Narrative*. New York: Columbia University Press, 1971. 143–72.

Daniels, Barry, ed. *Joseph Chaikin and Sam Shepard: Letters and Texts, 1972–84*. New York: NAL, 1989.

Davidson, Sara. "A Visit with Joan Didion." Friedman, *Joan Didion* 13–21.

de Lauretis, Teresa, ed. *Feminist Studies/Critical Studies*. Bloomington: Indiana University Press, 1986.

de Man, Paul. "Autobiography as De-facement." *MLN* 94.5 (1979): 919–30.

D'Erasmo, Stacey. "Loving Lillian." Rev. of *Hellman and Hammett: The Legendary Passion of Lillian Hellman and Dashiell Hammett*, by Joan Mellen. *The Nation* 24 June 1996: 25–27.

Dick, Bernard. *Hellman in Hollywood*. East Brunswick, N.J.: Associated University Presses, 1982.

Didion, Joan. *After Henry*. New York: Simon and Schuster, 1992.

_____. *A Book of Common Prayer*. New York: Pocket Books, 1977.

_____. *Miami*. New York: Simon and Schuster, 1987.

_____. *Slouching Towards Bethlehem*. New York: Washington Square, 1981.

_____. "Trouble in Lakewood." *The New Yorker* 26 July 1993: 46–65.

_____. *The White Album*. New York: Simon and Schuster, 1979.

Dixon, Melvin. *Ride Out the Wilderness: Geography and Identity in Afro-American Literature*. Urbana: University of Illinois Press, 1987.

Dydo, Ulla E. "Gertrude Stein: Composition as Meditation." Neuman and Nadel 42–60.

_____. "Landscape Is Not Grammar: Gertrude Stein in 1928." *Raritan* 7.1 (Summer 1987): 97–113.

_____. "*Stanzas in Meditation*: The Other Autobiography." *Chicago Review* 35.2 (1985): 4–20.

_____, ed. *A Stein Reader*. Evanston, Ill.: Northwestern University Press, 1993.

Eagleton, Terry. *Literary Theory: An Introduction*. Minneapolis: University of Minnesota Press, 1983.

Eakin, Paul John. *Fictions in Autobiography: Studies in the Art of Self-Invention*. Princeton, N.J.: Princeton University Press, 1985.

_____. "Narrative and Chronology as Structures of Reference and the New Model Autobiographer." Olney, *Studies* 32–41.

_____. *Touching the World: Reference in Autobiography*. Princeton, N.J.: Princeton University Press, 1992.

Early, Michael. "Of Life Immense in Passion, Pulse, and Power: Sam Shepard and the American Literary Tradition." Marranca, *American Dreams* 126–32.

Egan, Susanna. *Patterns of Experience in Autobiography*. Chapel Hill: University of North Carolina Press, 1984.

Elbaz, Robert. *The Changing Nature of the Self: A Critical Study of the Autobiographic Discourse*. Iowa City: University of Iowa Press, 1987.

Falk, Florence. "Men Without Women: The Shepard Landscape." Marranca, *American Dreams* 90–103.

Ferriss, Suzanne. Letter to the author. 5 Sept. 1995.

Fichtelberg, Joseph. *The Complex Image: Faith and Method in American Autobiography*. Philadelphia: University of Pennsylvania Press, 1989.

Fitzgerald, F. Scott. *The Great Gatsby*. New York: Scribner's, 1925.

Foley, Barbara. "Fact, Fiction, and Reality." *Contemporary Literature* 20.3 (1979): 389–99.

Foucault, Michel. "What Is an Author?" In *Textual Strategies: Perspectives in Post-Structuralist Criticism*. Ed. Josue V. Harari. Ithaca, N.Y.: Cornell University Press, 1979. 141–60.

Friedman, Ellen G. "The Didion Sensibility: An Analysis." Friedman, *Joan Didion* 81–90.

_____, ed. *Joan Didion: Essays and Conversations*. Princeton: Ontario Review Press, 1984.

Friedman, Susan Stanford. "Women's Autobiographical Selves: Theory and Practice." Benstock, *Private Self* 34–62.

Fuss, Diana. *Essentially Speaking: Feminism, Nature, and Difference*. New York: Routledge, 1989.

Gardiner, Judith Kegan. "On Female Identity and Writing by Women." *Critical Inquiry* 8 (Winter 1981): 347–61.

Gelber, Jack. "Sam Shepard: The Playwright as Shaman." Shepard, *Angel City and Other Plays* 1–4.

Gellhorn, Martha. "On Apocryphism." *Paris Review* 23 (Spring 1981): 280–301.

Gilman, Richard. Introduction. Shepard, *Seven Plays* ix–xxv.

Gilmore, Leigh. *Autobiographics: A Feminist Theory of Women's Self-Representation*. Ithaca, N.Y.: Cornell University Press, 1994.

_____. "The Mark of Autobiography: Postmodernism, Autobiography, and Genre." Ashley 3–18.

Glazer, Nathan. "An Answer to Lillian Hellman." *Commentary* 61 June 1976: 36–39.

Grant, Gary. "Writing as a Process of Performing the Self: Sam Shepard's Notebooks." *Modern Drama* 34.4 (Dec. 1991): 549–65.

Goodman, Ellen. "Autobiographies as Hot Art." *Miami Herald* 8 Apr. 1997: 11A.

Grossman, Anita Susan. "Art Versus Truth in Autobiography: The Case of Lillian Hellman." *CLIO: A Journal of Literature, History, and the Philosophy of History* 14.3 (Spring 1985): 289–308.

Gunn, Janet Varner. *Autobiography: Toward a Poetics of Experience*. Philadelphia: University of Pennsylvania Press, 1982.

Gusdorf, Georges. "Conditions and Limits of Autobiography." Olney, *Autobiography* 28–48.

Haas, Robert Bartlett, ed. *A Primer for the Gradual Understanding of Gertrude Stein*. Los Angeles: Black Sparrow Press, 1971.

Harrison, Gilbert, ed. *Gertrude Stein's America*. Washington, D.C.: Robert B. Luce, 1965.

Hart, Francis R. "Notes for an Anatomy of Modern Autobiography." In *New Directions in Literary History*. Ed. Ralph Cohen. Baltimore: Johns Hopkins University Press, 1974. 221–47.

Heller, Scott. "A Study Shows that Gertrude Stein Backed the Vichy Government During World War II." *Chronicle of Higher Education* 18 October 1996: A14–A16.

Hellman, John. "The Nature and Modes of the New Journalism: A Theory." *Genre* 13 (Winter 1980): 517–29.

Hellman, Lillian. *Another Part of the Forest*. New York: Viking, 1947.

_____. *The Autumn Garden*. In *Famous American Plays of the 1950s*. New York: Dell, 1962.

_____. *Four Plays by Lillian Hellman*. New York: Random, 1942.

_____. *Maybe, a Story*. Boston: Little, 1980.

_____. "On Jumping into Life." *Mademoiselle* Aug. 1975: 167.

_____. *Three*. Boston: Little, 1979.

_____. *Toys in the Attic*. New York: Random, 1960.

Hermann, Claudine. "Women in Space and Time." Trans. by Marilyn R.

Schuster. In *New French Feminisms: An Anthology*. Eds. Elaine Marks and Isabelle de Courtivron. New York: Schocken, 1981. 168–73.

Hersey, John. "Lillian Hellman." *The New Republic* 175 (18 September 1976): 25–27.

Hewitt, Leah Diane. Introduction. *Autobiographical Tightropes*. Lincoln: University of Nebraska Press, 1990.

Hook, Sidney. "Lillian Hellman's *Scoundrel Time*." *Encounter* 48 (Feb. 1977): 82–91.

Howarth, William L. "Some Principles of Autobiography." *New Literary History* 5.2 (Winter 1974): 363–81.

"Human Rights Watch/Free Expression Project: Hellman/Hammett Grants." *Poets and Writers Magazine* (Nov./Dec. 1994): 78.

Hummon, David M. "Place Identity: Localities of the Self." In *Proceedings of 1986 International Conference on Built Form and Culture Research*. Eds. William J. Carswell and David G. Saile. Lawrence: University of Kansas, n.d. 34–37.

Janeway, Elizabeth. "Women's Literature." In *Harvard Guide to Contemporary Writing*. Ed. Daniel Hoffmann. Cambridge, Mass.: Harvard University Press, Belknap Press, 1979. 342–95.

Jay, Gregory S. *America the Scrivener: Deconstruction and the Subject of Literary History*. Ithaca, N.Y.: Cornell University Press, 1990.

Jay, Paul L. "Being in the Text: Autobiography and the Problem of the Subject." *MLN* 97 (Dec. 1982): 1045–63.

_____. "Posing: Autobiography and the Subject of Photography." Ashley 191–211.

_____. "What's the Use?: Critical Theory and the Study of Autobiography." *Biography: An Interdisciplinary Quarterly* 10.1 (Winter 1987): 39–54.

Jelinek, Estelle C. "Introduction: Women's Autobiography and the Male Tradition." Jelinek, *Women's Autobiography* 1–20.

_____. "A Response to 'Shaping Women's Lives.'" *a/b: Auto/Biography Studies* 4.1 (Fall 1988): 23–26.

_____, ed. *Women's Autobiography: Essays in Criticism*. Bloomington: Indiana University Press, 1980.

Jones, Suzanne W. "Place, Perception, and Identity in *The Awakening*." In *Perspectives on Kate Chopin: Proceedings from the Kate Chopin International Conference*. April 6–8, 1989. Natchitoches, La.: Northwestern State University, 1992. 59–74.

Kakutani, Michiko. "The Freedom of Fiction, Applied to Biography." *New York Times* 23 Sept. 1990: B1+.

_____. "Joan Didion: Staking out California." In Friedman, *Joan Didion.* 29–40.

_____. "Myths, Dreams, Realities — Sam Shepard's America." *New York Times* 29 Jan. 1984, section 2.

Kazin, Alfred. "The Legend of Lillian Hellman." *Esquire* 88.2 (August 1977): 28, 30, 34.

_____. "The Self as History: Reflections on Autobiography." Pachter 73–89.

Kennedy, J. Gerald. *Imagining Paris: Exile, Writing, and American Identity.* New Haven, Conn.: Yale University Press, 1993.

_____. "Place, Self, and Writing." *Southern Review* 26 (Summer 1990): 496–516.

_____. "Roland Barthes, Autobiography, and the End of Writing." *Georgia Review* 35 (Summer 1981): 381–98.

Kimball, King. Introduction. *Sam Shepard: A Casebook.* Casebooks on Modern Dramatists 2. New York: Garland, 1988. ix–xviii.

Kirby, Kathleen M. "Thinking Through the Boundary: The Politics of Location, Subjects, and Space." *boundary 2: An International Journal of Literature and Culture* 20.2 (1993): 173–89.

Kopkind, Andrew. "Countrification." *The Nation* 27 Oct. 1984: 425–26.

Kracauer, Siegfried. "Photography." Trachtenberg 245–68.

Kramer, Hilton. "The Life and Death of Lillian Hellman." *The New Criterion* 3.2 (Oct. 1984): 1–6.

Kramer, Lloyd S. *Threshold of a New World: Intellectuals and the Exile Experience in Paris, 1830–1848.* Ithaca, N.Y.: Cornell University Press, 1988.

Kroll, Jack, Constance Gutherie, and Janet Huck. "Who's That Tall Dark Stranger?" *Newsweek* 11 Nov. 1985: 68–74.

Krupat, Arnold. "American Autobiography: The Western Tradition." *Georgia Review* 35 (1981): 307–17.

Lavin, Marjorie Woods, and Fredric Agatstein. "Personal Identity and the Imagery of Place: Psychological Issues and Literary Themes." *Journal of Mental Imagery* 8.3 (1984): 51–66.

Lederer, Katherine. *Lillian Hellman.* Boston: Twayne, 1979.

Lejeune, Philippe. "Autobiography in the Third Person." *New Literary History* 9 (1977): 27–50.

Lion, John. "Rock n' Roll Jesus with a Cowboy Mouth." *American Theatre* April 1984: 4–8.

Lippman, Amy. "Rhythm and Truths: An Interview with Sam Shepard." *American Theatre* April 1984: 9–13, 40–41.

Londre, Felicia Hardison. "Sam Shepard Works Out: The Masculinization of America." *Studies in American Drama, 1945–Present* 2 (1987): 19–27.

Lutwack, Leonard. *The Role of Place in Literature.* Syracuse, N.Y.: Syracuse University Press, 1984.

Marcus, Jane. "Invincible Mediocrity: The Private Selves of Public Women." Benstock, *Private Self* 114–46.

Marranca, Bonnie. "Alphabetical Shepard: The Play of Words." *American Dreams* 13–33.

_____, ed. *American Dreams: The Imagination of Sam Shepard.* New York: Performing Arts Journal Publications, 1981.

_____. Preface. Marranca, *American Dreams.*

Martin, William B. "Lillian Hellman's Table Talk." *Conference of College Teachers of English of Texas* 41 (Sept. 1981). Ed. Turner S. Kobler. 29–35.

Mason, Mary G., and Carol Hurd Greed, eds. *Journeys: Autobiographical Writings by Women.* Boston: G. K. Hall, 1979.

Mayne, Richard. "Ishmael and the Inquisitors." Rev. of *Scoundrel Time,* by Lillian Hellman. *Times Literary Supplement* 12 Nov. 1976: 1413.

McCracken, Samuel. "'Julia' and Other Fictions by Lillian Hellman." *Commentary* June 1984: 35–43.

Mellen, Joan. *Hellman and Hammett: The Legendary Passion of Lillian Hellman and Dashiell Hammett.* New York: Harper, 1996.

Merrill, Cynthia. "Mirrored Image: Gertrude Stein and Autobiography." *Pacific Coast Philology* 20.1–2 (Nov. 1985): 11–17.

Mohanty, Chandra Talpade. "Cartographies of Struggle." In *Third World Women and the Politics of Feminism.* Eds. Chandra Talpade Mohanty, Lordes Torres, and Ann Russo. Bloomington: Indiana University Press, 1991. 1–47.

Moi, Toril. *Sexual/Textual Politics: Feminist Literary Theory.* New York: Methuen, 1985.

Mottram, Ron. *Inner Landscapes: The Theater of Sam Shepard.* Columbia: University of Missouri Press, 1984.

Mowitt, John. Foreword. Paul Smith, *Discerning the Subject.* ix–xiii.

Navasky, Victor S. *Naming Names.* New York: Viking Press, 1980.

Neuman, Shirley C. *Gertrude Stein: Autobiography and the Problem of Narration.* ELS Monograph Series 18. Victoria, B.C.: University of Victoria, 1979.

_____. "Gertrude Stein's Dog: 'Personal Identity' and Autobiography." *Canadian Review of Comparative Literature* 10.1 (March 1983): 62–79.

Neuman, Shirley, and Ira B. Nadel, eds. *Gertrude Stein and the Making of Literature.* Boston: Northeastern University Press, 1988.

Nightingale, Peggy, ed. *A Sense of Place in the New Literatures in English.* St. Lucia and London: University of Queensland Press, 1986.

Nussbaum, Felicity A. *The Autobiographical Subject: Gender and Ideology in Eighteenth-Century England*. Baltimore: Johns Hopkins University Press, 1989.

_____. "Toward Conceptualizing Diary." Olney, *Studies* 128–40.

Olney, James. "Autobiography and the Cultural Movement: A Thematic, Historical, and Bibliographical Introduction." Olney, *Autobiography* 3–27.

_____, ed. *Autobiography: Essays Theoretical and Critical*. Princeton, N.J.: Princeton University Press, 1980.

_____. "Some Versions of Memory/Some Versions of *Bios*: The Ontology of Autobiography." Olney, *Autobiography* 236–267.

_____, ed. *Studies in Autobiography*. New York: Oxford University Press, 1988.

Oumano, Ellen. *Sam Shepard: The Life and Work of an American Dreamer*. New York: St. Martin's, 1986.

Pachter, Marc, ed. *Telling Lives: The Biographer's Art*. Philadelphia: University of Pennsylvania Press, 1981.

Parke, Catherine N. "'Simple Through Complication': Gertrude Stein Thinking." *American Literature* 60.4 (December 1988): 555–74.

Pascal, Roy. *Design and Truth in Autobiography*. Cambridge: Harvard University Press, 1960.

Relph, Edward. *Place and Placelessness*. London: Pion Ltd., 1976.

Renza, Louis A. "The Veto of the Imagination: A Theory of Autobiography." *New Literary History* 9.1 (Autumn 1977): 1–6.

Rollyson, Carl E. *Lillian Hellman: Her Legend and Her Legacy*. New York: St. Martin's, 1988.

Rosen, Carol. "'Emotional Territory': An Interview with Sam Shepard." *Modern Drama* 36.1 (March 1993): 1–11.

Ruddick, Lisa Cole. *Reading Gertrude Stein: Body, Text, Gnosis*. Reading Women Writing Series. Ithaca, N.Y.: Cornell University Press, 1990.

Russo, John Paul. "The Disappearance of the Self: Some Theories of Autobiography in the United States, 1964–1987." *Letterature D'America* 7.29–31 (1986–87): 5–42.

Sayre, Robert F. "The Proper Study — Autobiographies in American Studies." *American Quarterly* 29 (1977): 241–62.

Schiff, Stephen. "Shepard on Broadway." *The New Yorker* 22 Apr. 1996: 85.

Schmitz, Neil. "Portrait, Patriarchy, Mythos: The Revenge of Gertrude Stein." *Salmagundi* 40 (Winter 78): 69–91.

Shapiro, Stephen A. "The Dark Continent of Literature: Autobiography." *Comparative Literature Studies* 5 (1968): 421–54.

Shattan, Joseph. "Who's the Scoundrel?" *Midstream* 8 (22 Oct. 1976): 67–77.

Shepard, Sam. "American Experimental Theatre: Then and Now." Marranca, *American Dreams* 212–13.

_____. *Angel City and Other Plays.* New York: Applause, 1981.

_____. *Cruising Paradise.* New York: Knopf, 1996.

_____. *Fool for Love and Other Plays.* New York: Bantam, 1984.

_____. *Hawk Moon.* Los Angeles: Black Sparrow Press, 1973.

_____. "Language, Visualization, and the Inner Library." Marranca, *American Dreams* 214–19.

_____. *A Lie of the Mind.* New York: NAL, 1986.

_____. "Metaphors, Mad Dogs and Old Time Cowboys: Interview with Sam Shepard." With Kenneth Chubb and the Editors of *Theatre Quarterly*. Marranca, *American Dreams* 187–209.

_____. *Motel Chronicles.* San Francisco: City Lights, 1982.

_____. *The Rolling Thunder Logbook.* New York: Viking, 1977.

_____. *Seven Plays.* New York: Bantam, 1981.

_____. "Time." Marranca, *American Dreams* 210–11.

_____. *True Dylan. Esquire* July 1987: 59–68.

_____. *The Unseen Hand and Other Plays.* New York: Bantam, 1986.

Shewey, Don. *Sam Shepard: The Life, the Loves, Behind the Legend of a True American Original.* New York: Dell, 1985.

_____. "Sam Shepard's Identity Dance." *American Theatre* July/August 1997: 12+.

Smith, Patti. "9 Random Years [7 + 2]." Shepard, *Angel City and Other Plays* 241–45.

Smith, Paul. *Discerning the Subject.* Theory and History of Literature 55. Minneapolis: University of Minnesota Press, 1988.

Smith, Sidonie. "Identity's Body." Ashley 266–92.

_____. "The Impact of Critical Theory on the Study of Autobiography: Marginality, Gender, and Autobiographical Practice." *a/b: Auto/Biography Studies* 3.3 (Fall 1987): 1–12.

_____. *A Poetics of Women's Autobiography: Marginality and the Fictions of Self-Representation.* Bloomington: Indiana University Press, 1987.

_____. "Re-Citing, Re-Siting, and Re-Sighting Likeness: Reading the Family Archive in Drucilla Modjeska's *Poppy*, Donna Williams' *Nobody Nowhere*, and Sally Morgan's *My Place*." *Modern Fiction Studies* 40.3 (Fall 1994): 509–42.

_____. "Self, Subject, and Resistance: Marginalities and Twentieth-Century Autobiographical Practice." *Tulsa Studies in Women's Literature* 9.1 (Spring 1990): 11–24.

Spengemann, William C. *A Mirror for Americanists: Reflections on the Idea of American Literature*. Hanover, N.H.: University Press of New England, 1989.

Spengemann, William C., and L. R. Lundquist. "Autobiography and the American Myth." *American Quarterly* 17 (Feb. 1965): 501–19.

Sprinker, Michael. "Fictions of the Self: The End of Autobiography." Olney, *Autobiography* 321–42.

Stambolian, George. "A Trip Through Popular Culture: *Mad Dog Blues*." Marranca, *American Dreams* 79–89.

Stanton, Domna C., ed. *The Female Autograph: Theory and Practice of Autobiography from the Tenth to the Twentieth Century*. Chicago: University of Chicago Press, 1987.

Stein, Gertrude. *The Autobiography of Alice B. Toklas*. New York: Vintage, 1933.

_____. "Composition as Explanation." Van Vechten 512–23.

_____. *Everybody's Autobiography*. 1937. New York: Vintage, 1973.

_____. *How Writing Is Written*. Ed. Robert Bartlett Haas. The Previously Uncollected Writings of Gertrude Stein, Vol. 2. Los Angeles: Black Sparrow Press, 1974.

_____. *Narration: Four Lectures by Gertrude Stein*. Chicago: University of Chicago Press, 1935.

_____. *Paris France*. New York: Liveright, 1940.

_____. "A Transatlantic Interview —1946." Haas 11–35.

_____. *Wars I Have Seen*. New York: Random, 1945.

Stein, Leo. *Journey into the Self: Being the Letters, Papers and Journals of Leo Stein*. Ed. Edmund Fuller. New York: Crown, 1950.

Stone, Albert E. *Autobiographical Occasions and Original Acts: Versions of American Identity from Henry Adams to Nate Shaw*. Philadelphia: University of Pennsylvania Press, 1982.

Toklas, Alice B. *What Is Remembered*. New York: Holt, Rinehart and Winston, 1963.

Trachtenberg, Alan, ed. *Classic Essays on Photography*. New Haven: Leete's Island Books, 1980.

Tuan, Yi-Fu. *Space and Place: The Perspective of Experience*. Minneapolis: University of Minnesota Press, 1977.

Van Vechten, Carl, ed. *Selected Writings of Gertrude Stein*. New York: Vintage, 1972.

VerMeulen, Michael. "Sam Shepard: Yes, Yes, Yes." *Esquire* Feb. 1980: 79–86.

Wagner-Martin, Linda W. *"Favored Strangers": Gertrude Stein and Her Family*. New Brunswick, N.J.: Rutgers University Press, 1995.

_____. "Lillian Hellman: Autobiography and Truth." *Southern Review* 19.2 (Spring 1983): 275–88.

Warhol, Robyn R., and Diane Price Herndl, eds. *Feminisms: An Anthology of Literary Theory and Criticism*. New Brunswick, N.J.: Rutgers University Press, 1991.

Waterson, Elizabeth. "Prophetic Self and the Problem of Voice." *Canadian Review of American Studies* 13.2 (Fall 1982): 193–97.

Wetzsteon, Ross. "Sam Shepard: Escape Artist." *Partisan Review* 49.2 (1982): 253–61.

Whitman, Walt. *The Collected Writings of Walt Whitman*. Eds. Harold W. Blodgett and Sculley Bradley. New York: New York University Press, 1965.

Wilson, Ann. "Great Expectations: Language and the Problem of Presence in Sam Shepard's Writing." Kimball 135–53.

Winston, Elizabeth. "Gertrude Stein's Mediating Stanzas." *Biography* 9.3 (Summer 1986): 229–46.

Woodward, Kathleen. "Simone de Beauvoir: Aging and Its Discontents." Benstock, *Private Self* 90–113.

Wyatt, David. "Shepard's Split." *South Atlantic Quarterly* 91.2 (Winter 1992): 333–60.

York, Lorraine M. "'The Things That Are Seen in the Flashes': Timothy Findley's *Inside Memory* As Photographic Life Writing." *Modern Fiction Studies* 40.3 (Fall 1994): 643–56.

Index